THE ASTHMA HANDBOOK

Henry Middleton.

30/12/96

THE ASTHMA HANDBOOK

A definitive guide to the causes,
symptoms and all the latest treatments

Jenny Lewis

with the National Asthma Campaign

VERMILION

LONDON

First published 1995

1 3 5 7 9 10 8 6 4 2

First published in the United Kingdom in 1995 by Vermilion
an imprint of Ebury Press
Random House
20 Vauxhall Bridge Road
London SW1V 2SA

Random House Australia (Pty) Limited
20 Alfred Street, Milsons Point, Sydney,
New South Wales 2061, Australia

Random House New Zealand Limited
18 Poland Road, Glenfield,
Auckland 10, New Zealand

Random House South Africa (Pty) Limited
PO Box 337, Bergvlei, South Africa

Random House UK Limited Reg. No. 954009

A CIP catalogue record for this book is available from the British Library

ISBN: 0 09 180673 9

Typeset in Century Old Style by SX Composing, Rayleigh, Essex
Printed and bound in Great Britain by Mackays of Chatham, PLC

Papers used by Ebury Press are natural, recyclable products made
from wood grown in sustainable forests.

CONTENTS

FOREWORD

Over three million people in the UK now have asthma. At least one million of these are children, and 155 children end up in hospital every day because of their asthma. It is the only controllable chronic condition which is on the increase and it actually kills someone every four hours.

Many people with asthma suffer from reduced quality of life, and some are severely disabled by the condition. However, it is not all gloom and doom. The good news is that, for the majority of patients, asthma can be controlled. The key is understanding about the condition and a partnership approach between the patient and the doctor or nurse responsible for their care. Working in this way people with asthma can come to understand what it is that triggers their symptoms (this varies widely as asthma is a very complex condition) and can then develop a strategy for avoiding those triggers as far as possible. This, combined with judicious use of modern medication, should mean that many patients are able to live an almost symptom-free life. Some patients find that complementary treatments are also helpful, and these can be a useful adjunct to traditional medication, although at present there is no evidence that they can actually replace them.

Whether you have asthma yourself, are caring for an asthma patient, or are simply interested in how this common, and potentially very debilitating, condition can be brought under control, you will find much to advise and assist you in this important book.

Melinda Letts
Chief Executive
National Asthma Campaign

INTRODUCTION

The prevalence of asthma has doubled over the past 15 years. More than 3 million people have the condition in the UK – over one million of them school-age children. Today asthma is one of the most significant Western ailments. Why this illness is on the rise is not really known. The increase of pollutants in the atmosphere, cigarette smoke, higher standards of living in terms of centrally heated and carpeted homes are some of the many reasons cited. Environmental conditions certainly play an important part in triggering attacks in susceptible people. Also, asthma is better known. It is much more frequently diagnosed, so maybe we are getting to know of more asthma patients than were known in the past.

Asthma is the cause of over 100,000 hospital visits every year and 1,600 people died from the condition in 1993. The National Asthma Campaign believes that many of these visits and some of these lives could have been saved. Not only is medical treatment much more efficient in modern times but, equally importantly, today's asthma patients can be helped effectively to take most of their treatment into their own hands. If you have asthma you can, for the most part, look after your condition so well that serious attacks are rare, and if and when they do come along they can be handled with the minimum of stress or panic and almost always without the fear of losing your life.

If your child has asthma the same applies. Together you can start to understand the condition and, depending on age of course, he (or she) can learn to take some responsibility for it. If he goes on to have asthma as an adult the early training will be a lesson that will serve him well for the rest of his life. But even if the asthma goes, learning to take charge rather than be fearful is an ability we can all use even when we're fit and strong and riding high.

The word 'asthma' is derived from the Greek and it means 'panting' or 'gasping for breath'. The first mention of an asthma-like illness appeared over 3,500 years ago in Egypt in the *Embers Papyrus*. Since then we have come a long way in understanding the pathology of the condition and, of course, in treating it.

Writing in the January 1995 issue of *Asthma News*, the journal of the National Asthma Campaign, Kay Dempster notes: 'The greatest authority on asthma in Victorian England was Henry Salter, physician to the Charing Cross Hospital. He opposed the use of sedatives and recommended, amongst other things, the use of strong black coffee. He also noted that hay and the presence of animals could act as trigger factors.

'Developing the concept of allergy in asthma was one of the most significant breakthroughs. Reactions to foreign substances had been observed among people with asthma for centuries. For example, in 1547 feathers were warned against, in 1565 rose-sniffing was avoided and in 1786 attention was drawn to the danger of feather beds. It wasn't until the nineteenth century that these observations began to be linked.'

The first book on asthma is thought to have been written in 1190 by the Jewish physician Moses Maimonides. Kay Dempster writes: 'His concept of asthma was as confused as that of the Greeks before him, but he spent much time treating the asthmatic son of Sultan Saladin. He advised a dry climate, an even temper, avoidance of emotional turmoil (particularly sexual activity) and suggests that sufferers take chicken soup!'

Current thinking is a little different and so is this book! Written with the help and support of the National Asthma Campaign, it is designed to help asthma patients to take control of their condition and, in so doing, enjoy full and active lives. We believe that asthma is only a small part of you and we hope to help you keep it that way.

A little about the pathology of asthma is explained in Chapter 1. It may help you to know why your chest gets tight, your breath gets short or you wheeze or cough. Knowing the whys and wherefores can help you assess the implications of your symptoms at any given time. Understanding the treatments will not only tell you what the different drugs and inhalers do, but armed with this information you may be able to make choices that best suit you. Being aware of the different triggers may help you to identify the ones that cause your attacks. If you can minimize or even eliminate some of those, it will have a very positive effect on your health.

However, most important of all is a plan which enables you to monitor your asthma daily so that if the condition is getting worse or an attack is threatened you will know and be able to take evasive action. Devising a Personal Management Plan is the most important weapon in your war against the condition and how to do this is explained fully in Chapter 3. The book also discusses what to do in an emergency and how to deal with flare-ups. The different aspects of living with asthma in terms of school, work, holiday and pregnancy are also included.

There are separate chapters on babies and children with asthma. Some 50 per cent of children who have asthma go on to lose their symptoms, but some will get them back at some stage. Adults who develop asthma tend to have the condition all their lives, but they will experience times when they are symptom-free and other periods when it is more troublesome. **Most adults who regularly monitor their asthma**

can keep it under control and, to a large extent, out of their lives.

Asthma can be a very isolating illness. The fear of an attack, together with the feeling of ill-health and lethargy that can accompany the condition, can make many asthma patients feel that life has short-changed them. Some children experience teasing at school; many have their studies disrupted. Adults may lose their jobs and their earning potential. According to the National Asthma Campaign 'Industry and the state also pay the price. In 1992 it was estimated that asthma cost the country a total of £943 million in DHSS and DSS payments and lost productivity.'

One way of counteracting this isolation is by knowing that many other people who have the condition share the same feelings, difficulties and triumphs. Some of them have recounted their experiences of asthma for this book: they tell you how it affects their lives and how it makes them feel. You will probably find that many of the stories will strike a chord with you. Hopefully they will help you to accept that the people who are living normal, active lives inspite of their asthma can be counted not in their hundreds but in their thousands.

Bear in mind that although, frequently, asthma is not curable, it can be managed. Unless you suffer from a very severe form of the condition, you can prevent most attacks. Acknowledging that you have asthma and therefore can have an attack is a very important step in managing the condition.

As you read some of the stories in the book you will see that people often say that they didn't regard their deteriorating condition as being serious. Or they may say that they leave it longer than they should before taking action in the case of an attack. Denying the condition or deterioration in the asthma is what puts you at risk. Being aware of asthma as it affects you, recognising when it is getting worse and taking action to prevent it getting out of control will greatly reduce your chances of having a serious attack. It also means, for most people, that you can live your life as you choose without being afraid of an unexpected asthma attack. In other words, **you can be in control** and the most important word in this statement is 'you'!

1

THIS IS ASTHMA

Our lungs have hundreds of tiny airways that carry air to and from the body. In people with asthma the lining of these airways is inflamed. The muscles around the airways are caused to constrict and the constriction makes the airways narrower and the passage of air much more difficult. But this is not the whole story. The inflammation of the airways has other effects. It makes them sensitive and twitchy, which is why, potentially, you have symptoms. In addition to the soreness, the airways can also become swollen and produce sticky phlegm and/or the accompanying cough. So what with the narrowing of the airways, their soreness and the thick mucus that is produced you can see why breathing becomes such a problem.

Even people with a very mild form of asthma will have an inherent increased sensitivity in the lining of their airways. When conditions are good this predisposition may not be noticeable. But when the person with asthma finds himself in a situation which triggers the condition, that is, makes the inflammation worse, symptoms ensue.

For instance, if someone who has sensitive airways goes into a room filled with cigarette smoke they may well be affected by the irritant; whereas a person whose airways are perfectly normal, with no inflammation, will probably be unaffected. The already sensitive airways will react to the irritant (cigarette smoke): the lining of the airways will become inflamed, the muscles will go into spasm and the person will, at best, start to wheeze but could, in all likelihood, suffer an asthma attack.

The situation is similar with a substance to which an asthma sufferer may be allergic, such as cat dander. If such a person comes into contact with a cat, or is even in a room where a cat has been, this allergen can provoke symptoms of asthma or even an attack. An *allergen* is something that produces allergy in susceptible people. Someone who does not have asthma or is not sensitive to cat dander would not be affected in this way.

Atopic asthma is asthma that is allergy based and it usually starts in childhood. The condition is likely to be triggered by external allergens like the house-dust mite, pollen, cat dander, or irritants like cigarette smoke. The person may well have one of the other atopic conditions mentioned in Chapter 12 as well – particularly eczema.

Atopic people tend to make larger than usual amounts of antibodies called *immunoglobin E* or *IgE*. Antibodies defend the body against foreign substances, also known as allergens. When antibodies meet up with undesirable substances, they react, and with asthma patients, the already irritable airways become inflamed.

There is often a family history of one of the other associated atopic conditions – eczema, allergic rhinitis and hayfever – but it is not necessarily apparent. It has been estimated that as many as a third of all people would prove to be atopic (allergic) if tested. Yet not all of these people have asthma or any of the other atopic conditions mentioned. However, they do all share a predisposition to them.

Asthma that develops later in life is usually a variety known as 'intrinsic' asthma. Here the triggers are not so easy to identify but viral infection is thought to be one. Allergy may still be important but is not so easily identified. Patients may also experience benign polyps in the nose. However, a great number of patients have both types of asthma so identifying which one you have may not be as helpful as it seems.

Viral infections are one of the commonest triggers of asthma in all age groups. The reason why asthma so often accompanies viral conditions may be due to a combination of an allergic response and the effect of the virus.

So asthma is a condition to which you have a predisposition, probably because of family connections. It is very likely that you have inherited a tendency to have asthma as part of your genetic make-up. It is not infectious, contagious or viral. **You cannot give asthma to anyone, nor can anyone catch it from you under any circumstances whatsoever!**

· *Symptoms of asthma* ·

Asthma can sometimes be difficult to diagnose because some of the symptoms can be similar to other condition such as, for instance, chronic bronchitis, emphysema or cystic fibrosis. But the following guide will give you a good idea as to whether or not the symptoms you experience are asthma.

NB: *However, asthma must be medically diagnosed and treated. If you have asthma it needs to be noted on your medical records.*

You may have asthma if:

● **You are short of breath.** If you experience breathlessness after laughing or crying you may be asthmatic. People with asthma also often find that they cannot finish each breath without needing another. One asthma patient has described it like this. 'You breathe in but you can't push that air out, so because you then have to breathe again you take another tiny, shallow breath. Eventually you are choking.'

• **Exercise makes you breathless.** If physical exertion (running for a bus, going up flights of stairs, playing sports) makes you more breathless than it does other people, it could be asthma. But it could be another condition like emphysema or heart disease.

• **You wheeze.** If you can hear a whistling sound as you breathe this could be because of the increased irritability of the airways, as well as the phlegm that has been produced as a result of an allergic reaction. Wheezing can be an indication of asthma, particularly in children, but not all asthmatic children wheeze.

• **You feel tight-chested.** Some asthma patients describe this sensation as a tight band across their chests. Many people get chesty after a bad cold or a bout of flu, but with asthma recovery can be very slow or may not happen without special treatment.

• **You cough.** Recurrent coughing that can sometimes produce a yellow, green or white mucus may be a sign of asthma. Adults will cough up phlegm while children will swallow it and then be sick. The coughing, which is often accompanied by wheezing, can be particularly bad at night. Persistent coughing is a common symptom of asthma in children.

• **You react badly to cold air.** If you find yourself breathless, with a tight chest, wheezy or coughing in cold weather it could well be that you have asthma.

• **You react to some drugs.** Breathlessness can be experienced after taking certain types of medicine which are not suitable for asthma patients. These include aspirin, some medicines prescribed for heart diseases like beta-blockers, some drugs for arthritis, non-steroid anti-inflammatory drugs like *ibuprofen* and some eye drops used for treating glaucoma.

People with asthma should be wary of taking **beta-blockers.** These drugs slow the heart rate and lower the blood pressure. They have the opposite effect to asthma-relieving beta-agonists, explained in the next chapter. Beta-blockers can cause breathing difficulties. They have been known to trigger severe, even fatal, asthma attacks. So even if they have been prescribed to treat another condition, it would be advisable to speak to your doctor and say that you are concerned about taking them because of your asthma. He can then either put your mind at rest or prescribe something else. Beta-blockers are used to treat high blood pressure, migraine and they can also be used in eye drops to treat glaucoma.

NB: *All the above symptoms are an indication of asthma but may not be asthma. People may have all or just one of them.*

In addition to those described above, there are other symptoms which can prove troublesome. The most important of these are:

• **Chest discomfort or tightness.** This is a very common symptom of asthma and often occurs during an asthma attack because air that is not being released through the airways becomes trapped in the lungs. The lungs expand and the membranes surrounding them stretch, and this can be painful.

● **Nasal problems.** A runny nose and nasal congestion is often an accompanying feature of asthma. This can be caused by the swelling of the nasal passages or by nasal polyps already mentioned in this chapter. The latter can be treated either by medication or surgery. These polyps are non-cancerous.

● **Lethargy.** People often feel very tired and lethargic when their asthma is bad. This can be due to a diminished supply of oxygen to the body. On the other hand, if the asthma has been triggered by flu or cold or other viral condition, the tiredness could be an after-effect of the illness as well as of the asthma itself.

· *Diagnosing asthma* ·

● **Taking a history.** Any doctor or nurse who suspects you may have asthma will ask a series of questions to help make a diagnosis. Some of these questions may include asking you if you have any of the symptoms mentioned above. But what may be significant is whether there is a history of atopic illness in the family. Do any of your relatives have eczema, hay fever or allergic rhinitis (an allergic condition of the nose)? Do you? Also, do your symptoms appear when, for instance, you are in the garden, or in a very dusty atmosphere, or when pollution levels are high, or when you stroke the neighbour's cat,? In other words, are the symptoms triggered by an allergen or an irritant?

● **Peak-flow meter reading.** This is a way of finding out how the lungs are performing. You do this by blowing into a peak-flow meter. How fast you can blow is an indication of your lungs' performance. A high reading shows you are breathing well. A low reading is a sign that the airways are narrowing. A person with asthma may experience a variation in their lungs' performance by more than 15 per cent, often between morning and evening. This kind of variation in breathing is a very significant pointer to asthma. It is one of the doctor's most important diagnostic tools.

If asthma is suspected and you are over the age of six, you will almost certainly be asked to blow into a peak-flow meter. Peak-flow varies according to a person's age, height and sex. To have a 'normal' peak-flow would mean that it would have to be within 20 per cent of someone who doesn't have asthma but is of the same sex, age and height as you. You may also be given a peak-flow meter to take home with you and asked to keep a diary to record your meter readings.

Peak-flow meters are not only an excellent way of diagnosing asthma, they are also essential in monitoring the condition which in turn can help you keep it under control. What they are and how to use them is described in Chapter 3

● **Anti-asthma medicine.** Sometimes doctors have to try anti-asthma drugs to confirm the diagnosis. Drugs prescribed for asthma are designed to improve your peak-flow and, of course, clear the symptoms. If this happens as a result of treatment, the diagnosis of asthma is confirmed. But it may mean taking the medicines for a few weeks before results are achieved and the diagnosis confirmed.

· *Levels of severity* ·

Asthma is a very individual illness. Different things trigger the condition in different people and the level of severity differs from person to person. Some patients will hardly be aware that they have asthma for most of their lives and only experience a few mild attacks now and again. Others will be aware of the condition somewhere in the background but so long as they monitor their breathing, take regular medication, and minimize the triggers they will lead full lives and experience very few flare-ups. But there are people with severe asthma who are aware of the condition all the time. They may lead limited lives, experience repeated attacks and they are continually being hospitalised. Fortunately it is rare for people to experience this level of severity.

Anyone's asthma can change from one level to another. So asthma regarded as severe today does not always stay that way. This is why it is important to have regular check-ups with your doctor or asthma nurse. The level of severity can go up or down and the medication needs to be adjusted accordingly.

● **Level one:** If you hardly ever experience symptoms except when you are doing physical exercise or are in very cold weather, the chances are that the linings of your airways are only slightly inflamed and your asthma is mild. Obviously if you can cut out some of the triggers described in Chapter 5, you may keep the condition at bay. You will not need preventative treatment but it is advisable to carry a *bronchodilator* with you all the time (you never know when you might have to run for a bus or exert yourself in some way that has not been planned). Bronchodilators open up the airways and as such they are known as 'relievers'. They are explained in Chapter 2.

● **Level two:** Although, by and large, you can get on with your life, the condition will fluctuate in severity from time to time, maybe even on a daily basis. The airways are sensitive and linings inflamed and although the flare-ups, when they come, are unlikely to be so severe that you are rushed off to hospital, you will react to triggers and your asthma will surely make its presence felt when you have a cold or flu. If your asthma is at this level, you really can play a very big part in keeping it under control. You will undoubtedly have been given reliever treatments but in addition you may well need to take some form of regular preventative medication as well. (These are described in Chapter 2).

If you can discipline yourself to keep a chart and take a regular peak-flow reading of your breathing morning and night, you will be able to spot a deterioration in your condition before it gets out of control. When the reading is up, you know you are well, when it is down you can heed the warning and, perhaps, increase the preventer dose. This management plan is something that you should discuss with your doctor or asthma nurse, but the essence of it is explained in Chapter 3. If you take your asthma seriously, monitor the condition and take the necessary medication, there is no reason why asthma should interfere with your life. Serious attacks should be a rare phenomenon.

● **Level three:** If asthma rules your life to the extent that you wake up wheezing and coughing in the night and it interferes with your daily routine, you obviously have a more severe form of the condition. Your attacks may lead to your being rushed into hospital for emergency treatment and you may even be hospitalised from time to time. Following attacks, you will be given steroid tablets to bring the condition under control, and in addition to the relievers you will certainly have to take preventative treatment daily to try and keep the asthma at bay. Again, monitoring your breathing with the aid of a peak-flow meter is a must. Asthma for you is a serious condition but it doesn't have to spoil your life. If you can take control, learn to recognise what constitutes, for you, good breathing, and be aware of any decline, you will often be able to stop a bad attack from happening. Equally, if you know what to do when an emergency arises without panicking, you may be able to take some of the fear out of the condition, reduce the stress it causes and maybe lower the severity of your asthma. What to do in an emergency is explained in Chapter 4.

● **Brittle asthma** is an extremely severe form of the condition which fortunately affects very few people with asthma. It is explained in Chapter 11 which includes the personal accounts of two brittle asthma sufferers.

But here are two stories of people with the usual form of the condition.

· HELEN ·

I was first diagnosed with asthma when I was 10 years old. That was 40 years ago. I can remember the first attack I had. We were staying with my grandmother in Kent and we'd gone to the seaside. It was a very windy day. We were having fish and chips and I had my first attack after that. I think I ate too much and the cold wind finished me off. Even now if I have a large meal I get short of breath. I had two more attacks of asthma when I visited my grandmother and her local GP banned us from going to see her. He said that I couldn't go there if I kept getting asthma attacks. I'm not sure what brought it on but it might have been stress to some extent. My mother was a terrible time-keeper and we always intended to set out first thing in the morning but never did. We never got going until the afternoon and I think the hanging around with nothing to do brought on the asthma. Anyway, we didn't visit my grandmother for several years afterwards.

When I was in my teens I would have attacks every four to six weeks. They never found out what triggered them. I missed a lot of schooling. At one time, when I was about 16 years old I was in the Maudsley Hospital. My doctor had tried everything he could for my asthma and it was thought at that time that asthma was a psychosomatic disease, that is, a physical disease with an emotional origin. I can't say that I particularly agreed with that but at the time I was prepared to try anything. Since I lived so far from the hospital I was admitted as an in-patient. I was there for the length of a school term. I saw a psychiatrist several times a week. It was this business of talking about whatever came into your mind. They took me off all my medication. During this time I had one attack. The sister on duty refused to give me anything for the attack. She told me I wasn't bad enough. I had to stay still. I couldn't move around because it made me breathless. The shift changed and the nurse who came on next gave me treatment for the attack.

I don't think the Maudsley Hospital's treatment made any difference to my asthma once I was out in the real world. I went back to the doctor who put me on steroid tablets (there weren't any inhaled ones then) and from then on my asthma was much better controlled. I went on to do A levels and eventually got my degree in nutrition at London University. I was on steroid tablets for about 10 years but towards the end the dose was very low.

I think my asthma has got worse over the years but the treatment has got better. In my teens I had quite a few bad attacks whereas now I don't get them at all, but the asthma is there in the background. But I take a preventer, a long-term bronchodilator and I carry around a reliever.

My attacks tended to build up gradually. They didn't just happen in a matter of minutes or even hours. It was more a question of a couple of days. Now the asthma is kept out of the attack stage because of the steroid preventer inhaler that I take and the long-term preventer. I don't believe in keeping my medicines to a minimum and only taking them when I'm in trouble. I take enough of the drugs to keep my asthma at a level where I don't get an attack.

My daughter was diagnosed with asthma when she was six years old. It took two or three years before we were able to get her on to a medication regime that would keep her asthma under control. Because I was asthmatic I knew what to look out for and I could question the doctors better. But seeing her during an attack was very painful. I knew what she was going through and I wanted to do more than I could. I think that's what made it so difficult. It also brought back memories for me and made me relive them when I saw her. I often had to leave the room and let my husband deal with it and it wasn't until later that I found out that he dealt with it by shutting it out of his mind!

She is 17 years old now and studying for her A levels. She is in charge of her own asthma medicines. Now that it is under control it might only be two or three days in a term that she is bad.

A couple of years ago she went on an adventure holiday. Amongst other things they climbed a mountain and went caving. It was February and the weather was cold. It rained a lot and I think it even snowed. I was very circumspect about letting her go. We wrote a letter explaining her treatment and sent her with duplicate medicines in case she lost any. I was nervous but she was fine. She did everything. She had no problems. I did worry but she has to be allowed to do these things.

· ELIZABETH ·

The very first time I had asthma I was about 12 years old. I had been knocked off my bicycle by a car. I wasn't hurt, just scared, and I had an attack straight away. I didn't have asthma for a long time after that until I was about 15. Then various things would set it off – cold weather, being overtired, laughing, or a viral infection. I don't remember it wrecking my life. I do remember being very wheezy and not being able to sleep and having to do deep breathing. But I wasn't incapacitated by it.

I got much better and I was all right during my twenties. The first time I had a really bad attack was when I was in my thirties. We'd been to a party. It was in the winter and it was in quite an old house. Old houses can set it off sometimes. I don't know whether it was that or if it was to do with coming out of a warm house into a cold atmosphere. I drove home and by the time I got home I was really quite breathless. It gradually got worse and the sheer effort of getting into bed was too much and I was taken into hospital for about three days. I was then put on to Becotide. I now take Becotide twice a day and Ventolin four times a day if I need it.

After that I was quite asthmatic for quite a while. I wasn't wheezy all the time but it didn't take much to set it off. These days my asthma is not chronic but it's acute. If I get an attack I get a bad one.

I became unconscious during one of my attacks. I'd been to a lovely party but I'd been wearing a strapless dress that was slightly constricting. I began to get wheezy so I came home a bit early and went to bed. I used the Ventolin but it didn't help and my husband called the doctor. A very young and very pretty doctor came. She was scared out of her wits. I was given a cortisone injection and she also brought a nebuliser. I can remember vaguely losing consciousness because I can remember somebody pulling my head up which was right down by my chest. I felt as if I was drenched in sweat. I was vaguely aware of people coming in and out of the room. I can remember one of my children being very distressed and feeling sad because I could not comfort her. At times I could hear my husband telling me to breathe but I felt that I didn't want to bother any more. The next thing I can remember is coming round in the hospital.

You breathe in but you can't push that air out. So, because you then have to breathe again you take another tiny shallow breath so eventually you are choking I suppose. You are just starving yourself of oxygen because you are not breathing out or breathing in again properly. In a sense it's like holding your breath until you pass out. It's very frightening.

The last attack I had was on Christmas night. All the children were coming home for Christmas and I was having Christmas lunch for 12 followed by lunch on Boxing Day for 24. I've been doing this kind of entertaining for a long time and outwardly it doesn't make me feel anxious but I guess internally it must do.

We'd had a lovely dinner on Christmas Eve. We'd had some wine and it may have been something to do with that because my husband said he felt ill in the morning. I had been fine until then. I think some wine has more sulphates which can affect asthmatics.

But I woke up on Christmas morning feeling slightly constricted. So I didn't go to church. I thought I'd stay quiet. It had been very cold on the Saturday here, having been mild up until then. It was a very foggy, freezing day. Everything was organised and ready for lunch. The others went to church and I just did one or two things in a leisurely way. When they returned we opened our presents and had lunch. Later on other people arrived and that was all fine and then at about 5.30 we sat down to watch television in our little study. There were quite a lot of people crammed into one room together, I expect, with a couple of cats and the dog. So after all that I thought I would go up to my bedroom which I have made very dust-free. It has a polished wood floor and it's quite simple with very little furniture. It's my asthma bolt-hole.

I now have a nebuliser. So I used that and felt a bit better and had a bit of a sleep. But by about 9.30 that evening I was bad again. I had used another nebuliser which didn't work. By now I knew I was not going to be able to control the attack. So I was driven to hospital.

They gave me a drip of aminophylline and oxygen and they did a blood test. They take blood from an artery so they can measure the amount of oxygen that is in your blood. That was Sunday night and I stayed in until Thursday morning.

Of course I missed the big get-together on Boxing Day which was disappointing. With three of my children grown up and left home it is not often that we are all together; but at Christmas all four girls were home and it was sad that I couldn't be there with them.

I suppose it has affected my life in that I've missed things. I've put a strain on my family. It's distressing for everybody. I've missed New Year's Eve parties and Christmases but nothing so far, luckily, that I haven't been able to think 'There'll be another time.' I didn't have asthma at my daughter's wedding or at my grandson's christening or at any of those one-off events. It's affected my life but it certainly hasn't wrecked it. And it doesn't stop me from doing things. When I'm well I can run, play tennis and do whatever I want to do. When I'm not having an attack I don't think about it.

2

TREATMENTS

There are a variety of sophisticated medicines currently available to treat asthma. However, the best treatment does not involve medicine at all. It comes under the heading of 'avoidance' and everything you need to know about it appears in Chapter 5. Avoiding the things that inflame your airways, aggravate the condition and set off an attack is obviously the best thing you can do for your asthma. It is not always easy. Sometimes you just cannot avoid the triggers. But there are many situations and occasions when you can, if you have the will and determination to do so – though it may well involve making difficult choices.

For instance, it may be hard on your partner to be asked never to smoke in your presence or in the house. Passive smoking on a regular basis will keep your airways constantly inflamed. Your asthma could deteriorate to a point where it becomes chronic and difficult to treat. So what do you do? Give your partner an easy time or your lungs a break?

Or maybe your household includes a much loved cat which distributes its dander all over the carpets, cushions, couches and bedding. Cat dander is a known allergen for asthma so it could well be affecting you. Do you put yourself through the emotional upheaval of giving away the cat, knowing that in time your lungs will thank you for it? Or do you stroke the mog and reach for the treatment?

This issue of asthma avoidance is very real and one that you need to consider seriously. So please read Chapter 5 on asthma triggers. If your asthma is mild it may be that all you have to do, most of the time, is to steer clear of some of the things that set it off. Medication will just be an occasional affair. Avoiding the avoidable allergens will certainly cut down on the amount of medicines you need to use – most of the time. And that's got to be a bonus.

But, having said that, it must also be stated that medicines play a very important part in asthma. There is no doubt that the judicious use of medicine will keep your asthma under control. This means taking the right amount of medicine for your particular needs. Taking a little bit less will keep your asthma short of being well-managed and leave you vulnerable to flare-ups. And you certainly don't want to go for the overkill. Getting your medication right is of paramount importance and you cannot do it in an arbitrary, haphazard way. You need to get medical help and this can come in the shape of your doctor, specialist or asthma nurse.

This does not mean that you have to accept blindly what you are told and take what you are given. It's your asthma and you need to be in the driving seat, but to be there you need to know what the drugs are and understand what they do.

Basically, there are three types of drugs. There are the **Preventers** which, as the name implies, work to prevent the asthma from happening. They do this by protecting the lining of the airways, stopping them from becoming inflamed or, if the asthma is chronic, keeping the inflammation down. This, in turn, reduces the mucus and the swelling and keeps the airways open. Different drugs do this in different ways and these are explained further on in this chapter.

Quick-acting relievers, also true to their name, relieve the situation when it arises. They are the rescue team that work by relaxing the muscles surrounding the airways. They dilate, or in other words, open up, the constricted bronchi (airways). This is why these medicines are known as *bronchodilators*. They help restore normal breathing. They do not protect the airways or help prevent attacks. When inhaled this type of reliever usually works within five to ten minutes and the effects last for about four hours. You use them when you need them to get you out of trouble and that's the best they can do for you!

NB: *You can always tell which is your reliever inhaler because the device is coloured blue.*

Long-acting relievers are similar to the relievers already described in that they open up the airways but they have a slightly different task. They are not quick-acting.The benefits take more time to be noticed – sometimes several days – but the effects last much longer. So they are not used for rescue work but are invaluable in keeping the airways open on a permanent basis. However, they do not effect the irritability or inflammation present in the airways. They are a type of bronchodilator with a different working mechanism. They don't prevent an attack and, strictly speaking, they don't treat one, but they protect you by keeping your airways open. However, these relievers should never be used instead of preventers. Some patients do use them as well as preventers but, as a rule of thumb, it is preferable to go on to a higher dose of preventer rather than take long-acting relievers.

Drugs in general use are known by three different names. The first one is the official medical one and it is a generic term for the basic active substance of the drug.

Secondly, different manufacturers will give different trade names to a drug which has the same basic active substance. This is to put their name on it so to speak. But the brand name is also the one that is usually easier to remember and say. '*Intal*', for instance, slips more easily off the tongue than '*sodium cromoglycate*' which is its generic name. When first referring to a drug I will give you both the brand and generic names, but after that I will just refer to the generic name since there are so many different brands. You can always find the generic name on your inhaler no matter what type it is. Look for the brand name and underneath it will tell you what the active substance is. So, for instance, under the word *'Bricanyl'*, you will see, probably in smaller letters, the word *'terbutaline'* which is its generic name.

Sometimes the basic substance of a drug may be combined with other substances to produce a slightly different medication and this may give it another name.

The third name a drug receives is the chemical and technical one. This consists of a mixture of letters and numbers which are mysterious to anyone outside the medical profession. Fortunately for us we don't need to worry about this!

Also, drugs are given different trade names in other countries. For instance, *salbutamol* is known as *albuterol* in America and we in the UK refer to *Turbohaler* whereas it is known as *Turbuhaler* in the rest of the world.

NB: *The drugs listed in the following pages are only some of the ones that are available and commonly prescribed. They are given as examples and are in no way intended to indicate recommendation or preference.*

· *Preventers* ·

Drugs in this category include: *Intal (sodium cromoglycate); Tilade (nedocromil); Becotide, Becloforte* (both are trade names for different strengths of *beclomethasone*); *Pulmicort (budesonide); Flixotide (fluticasone).*

Sodium cromoglycate and *nedocromil* are non-steroid anti-inflammatory drugs. They work by blocking off the allergic reaction as it occurs in the lungs. These drugs also damp down inflammation but, like steroids, do not effect a cure. There are no significant side-effects with these drugs. Steroid inhalers are prescribed more often these days than *sodium cromoglycate* or *nedocromil* because they are more effective.

Steroids are a group of natural hormones produced by the body. Among other functions they help the healing process. Artificially produced steroids aim to have the same effect. *Beclomethasone, budesonide* and *fluticasone* are steroid medicines. In the case of asthma, steroid treatment aims to reduce the inflammation in the airways. This healing process takes time which is why you have to take the drugs on a regular basis. Evidence suggests that there is inflammation present in the lungs which is potentially damaging to the lungs and which can produce an attack even when there are no symptoms present and the patient is feeling well.

Generally these preventers are taken in the form of an inhaler. This way the drug gets directly to the part of the body that needs it – the lungs. In this way you can aim to achieve the maximum effect with the minimum drug dosage. It also means that the drug isn't taken into the body in anywhere near the same quantity as it would be if you were swallowing a pill. A minuscule amount of the inhaled steroid is taken into the system which, of course, means that the side-effects are negligible, particularly if the dosage is low.

One possible side-effect is a sore mouth or throat. This is caused by thrush which is a fungal infection. A residual amount of the inhaled steroid remains in the mouth. This can have the effect of killing off the natural bacteria which keeps the mouth healthy. Thrush is easily treated. You may also experience a hoarseness in the voice. You can try and counteract this by brushing your teeth, rinsing, gargling and spitting the water out after you've used the inhaler which will remove the powder residue from your mouth. Both these side-effects tend to appear only on the higher doses of inhaled steroid. If problems persist speak to your doctor or nurse who may suggest changing the method of delivery of your medicine.

The most important thing to know about preventative treatment is that you must take the prescribed dose regularly. If you are on *sodium cromoglycate (Intal)* this will probably mean using the inhaler four times a day and sometimes before exercise. With *nedocromil sodium (Tilade)* the dose is usually twice a day. With the steroids you should only need to inhale twice a day. Please remember that this is whether you have symptoms of asthma or not. If you are on the steroid inhalers and you forget to take the treatment one day, you can double the dose the next day, particularly if you can feel a deterioration in the condition.

When the asthma is out of control steroids may be prescribed in tablet form. The drug prescribed is likely to be *Prednisolone*. This is a corticosteroid which reduces the inflammation and swelling in the lungs as well the amount of the mucus produced. Corticosteroids are quite different to the anabolic steroids used by some athletes and body builders. Many people worry about taking steroids, and not without cause. Corticosteroids can and do have unwanted side-effects when taken in sufficient quantity over a longer period of time. But severe asthma is no joy-trip either! These tablets are usually prescribed when the condition has become severe. To get the maximum effect you need to take a high dose for the time it takes to bring the inflammation down and get the condition under control. This can take from three to fourteen days. So taking less than the prescribed dose is not a good idea. Better to take the treatment and knock the flare-up on the head and then go back to your normal regime. Taken in short sharp bursts these steroids rarely have any lasting side-effects.

Taking *Prednisolone* in daily doses of 5mg or less may not cause any side-effects, even if taken regularly over many years. However, higher doses taken long term can have significant side-effects. You may put on weight and find you have a 'moon face' appearance. The drug can increase your blood pressure. It can also increase your chances of getting a peptic ulcer. Taken for long periods it can thin the bones which of course can make you more prone to osteoporosis.

In providing the body with an increased amount of artificial steroid (the hormone that helps the healing process), these steroids suppress the body's own steroid-producing mechanism. The body is getting all it needs from elsewhere (the tablets) and can stop producing its own. This can have serious consequences in the case of an accident or injury. Normally, in these circumstances the body would go into overdrive and produce extra amounts of steroid to help recovery. If you have been on a medium-to-high dose of steroids for some time this may not happen. So you have to take extra artificial steroids in these circumstances to help cope with the stress. This is why it is so important to carry a card saying you are on steroid tablets. If you are in an accident, medical staff will know that they may have to give you steroids, along with anything else they may have to do, because your body will need extra steroids if you are to recover.

It is also very important to know that if you have been on steroid tablets for more than a few weeks you have to come off them gradually and under medical supervision. The body needs time to adjust to the withdrawal of the steroid and removing them suddenly could make you very ill.

All this may sound alarming and taking steroids over a long period of time is not something that the medical profession generally subscribes to unless there is no other choice. Severe asthma is a serious and dangerous condition which may, at times, threaten your life. So you have to try and find a balance between the drugs and the condition and neither of them are happy options. In these circumstances you could be forgiven for feeling that you are somewhere between a rock and a hard place. This is why it is important to look at the trigger factors and try to avoid them and to concentrate on controlling the condition.

· *Quick-acting relievers* ·

These drugs include *Ventolin, Aerolin, Salbulin* (generically named *salbutamol* but produced by different drug manufacturers) and *Bricanyl (terbutaline)*. They are, as I've said before, the rescue team that dilate the airways and get you breathing. Their effects last for up to four hours and the most common side-effect is tremor in the hands. These drugs are based on adrenaline, a substance produced by the adrenal glands in times of stress or, of course, when taking exercise. The adrenaline opens up the airways and makes the heart beat faster, preparing the body for action.

These adrenaline-based bronchodilators are known as *beta-agonists* and they work by relaxing the muscles that surround the airways. They do not bring down the inflammation or swelling so do not in any way effect a cure. You only take them to counteract symptoms or before exercise. As a general rule you should not need to use these drugs more than once a day, other than for short periods when, for example, you have a cold. In these circumstances they can be used regularly for two or three days. Under normal circumstances if you find you are using them more than that, take it as an indication that your asthma may be getting worse or is out of control. To counteract this, examine the use of your preventer drug – have you been taking it regularly as prescribed? If not, that could be the answer. If you have been keeping to the management schedule, it may mean that you will have to step up the dose of your preventer treatment, at least for a while.

The other thing to think about is the trigger factor. Is there something you could avoid out there? There is no point in increasing the dose of your reliever drug if it will not bring the condition under control.

· *Long-acting relievers* ·

These drugs include: *Serevent (salmeterol)* and *Oxivent (oxitropium)*. *Serevent* is a longer acting beta-agonist bronchodilator. It keeps the airways open, but it acts more slowly and lasts longer – up to 12 hours. A possible side-effect of *Serevent* is trembling hands, and taken in high doses it can raise the pulse rate and cause heart palpitations. Although unpleasant, these reactions are not thought to be dangerous, but it obviously makes sense to take the minimum amount to keep the condition under control.

Oxivent is an *anticholinergic* bronchodilator. It blocks the effect of the cholinergic nerves that can, amongst other things, constrict the airways. This medicine has a limited function in that it only works on the cholinergic nerves and with most asthma patients the constriction is caused by several things. The side-effects of *Oxivent* may include dry mouths and very occasionally blurred vision.

Slo-Phyllin and *Uniphyllin* (*theophylline* is the generic name for both of these medicines) are protectors in tablet or syrup form. *Theophylline* is a caffeine-like substance and it is a long-acting bronchodilator. Its main advantage is that since it keeps the airways open for several hours it is a useful treatment for asthma patients to take at night. The flip side is in its side-effects. It can cause nausea, vomiting, indigestion, headaches and a feeling of anxiousness (as you might get if you were drinking too much coffee). These reactions are usually experienced when the levels of the drug in the blood are too high. Therefore anyone taking this medicine may need regular blood tests to monitor a good level.

· *Inhalers* ·

The most effective way of treating asthma is by putting the medication straight into the lungs, which is where the condition starts. This is done by means of an inhaler, and 34 different inhalers work best for different people. It is important to find the one that suits you best. It is thought that many people fail to get their asthma under control because they are not using their inhalers correctly. Inhalers are used for preventer and reliever treatment.

· *Devices* ·

Aerosol Inhalers are the most commonly used for both preventer and reliever treatment. They are also known as metered dose inhalers. The medicine is a fine powder mixed with a highly evaporative liquid contained in a miniature aerosol. The aerosol fits into a plastic activator. To operate the inhaler you push the top of the aerosol and the liquid is forced out through the plastic mouthpiece. It evaporates rapidly so that what you actually inhale is the fine powder. Each push delivers a metered dose of the drug. But you do have to get the coordination right, pressing down the canister as you breathe in. This technique is explained as follows by the National Asthma Campaign:

- Stand up (if possible).
- Remove the cap and then shake the inhaler.
- Tip your head back as far as you can. This stops too much of the medicine sticking to the back of your throat.
- Breathe out gently.
- Close your lips firmly around the inhaler mouthpiece and breathe in slowly, pressing the canister down as you continue to fill your lungs.
- Count ten seconds before breathing out again.

Autohaler is a type of aerosol inhaler which works by automatically releasing the medicine as you breathe in. No coordination is involved, which makes it a very useful device for children, the elderly and people with arthritis. It is more expensive than the other type of inhalers which

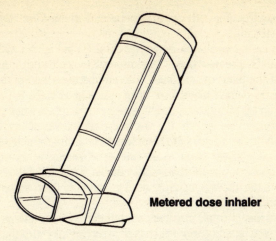

Metered dose inhaler

is why it is not prescribed as a matter of course. However, if you find you are not able to use your inhaler properly, it is well worth asking the doctor about this one.

Spacers are an add-on to the aerosol inhaler. Made of clear plastic, they usually come in two halves which fit together. The spacer is connected to the aerosol's mouthpiece. It mixes the medicine that is squirted out with air and holds it until you are ready to inhale. Spacers make the inhaler much easier to use because they have a valve system which allows you to inhale the medicine as you breathe in. When you breathe out the valve diverts the exhaled breath away from the chamber. You breathe in again and the valve allows the medicine mixture back into your lungs so you don't have to coordinate all the actions. If you are short of breath, simply breathe in and out as well as you can, putting one

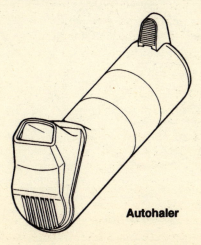

Autohaler

puff (or squirt) at a time into the spacer and shaking the canister between each puff.

Spacers are an invaluable device for children, but adults with asthma are also advised to use them. They improve the delivery of the drug to the lung. By mixing the medicine with air and allowing you to breathe naturally, the device delivers the drug into your airways without accumulating on the mouth and throat which may happen when you use a simple inhaler. This reduces the risk of the side-effects of steroids in the mouth and throat. Spacers are also extremely useful for delivering high doses of the reliever drug to anyone experiencing a severe asthma attack. A mask to fit the spacer is available for small children. Young children, under the age of four, need a mask as they cannot use the mouthpiece on a spacer.

Not all spacers fit all inhalers as the latter come in different shapes and sizes. You should check which type is correct for your inhaler before your doctor prescribes it.

Spacers are available on prescription but you can buy some, which fit many inhalers, from pharmacists without a prescription. In any event someone in the health care team, doctor, nurse or pharmacist, should check that you are using it correctly.

The **Aerochamber** is a spacer that can be more suitable for children.

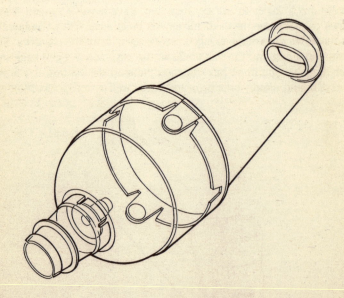

Spacer device

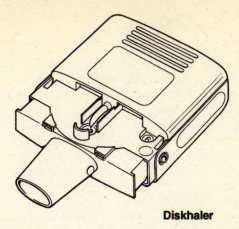

Diskhaler

Parents find it easier to hold with one hand as it is smaller. It comes in different sizes: baby, child and adult and includes a mask, and it fits all inhalers. But it is not available on prescription.

Makeshift spacers can be devised very quickly in an emergency when you do not have the real thing to hand. Take a large disposable drinking cup. Make a hole in the bottom of it and push the mouthpiece of the aerosol through it. This should create an air chamber into which the medicine can be puffed. You use the open end of the cup like a mask. This do-it-yourself spacer does not, of course, have the advantage of the valve system but it creates the airspace which traps the medicine, allowing you to breathe in and out without worrying about coordination. This can obviously take some of the panic out of a sudden or severe attack.

Powder Inhalers dispense the medicine in dry powder form. The drug is contained either in a single capsule, a disk cartridge containing

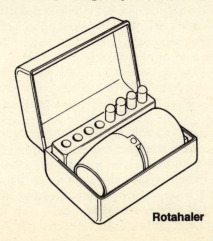

Rotahaler

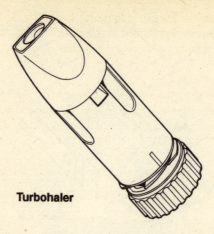

Turbohaler

several capsules or pre-packed in a compartment within the inhaler. As you breathe in, the powder is released into the lungs. Again it comes in a metered dose but coordination is not a factor. However, in the devices such as the Rotahaler, where the capsules have to be inserted one at a time, some people can find this fiddly. Examples of the powder inhalers are the *Diskhaler, Rotahaler* (see page 23) and *Turbohaler*.

Nebulisers deliver a high dose of the drug – usually a reliever. Nebulisers are used for emergency medical treatment. The drug that is put through the nebuliser is in a liquid form. The nebuliser has an air compressor. It forces air through the liquid which turns into a fine mist which you then breathe in through the mask. They deliver a dose which is 25 to 50 times stronger than an inhaler, which is why they appear so efficient. They usually relieve an attack very quickly. You can get portable nebulisers which have rechargeable batteries.

However, as a general rule it is not recommended that people have them at home unless the asthma is chronic and they are needed every day as part of a maintenance plan. People can put a lot of faith in the nebuliser because the relief is so immediate. But a nebuliser that gives a reliever dose is not treating the asthma. All it is doing is opening the airways. It is far more important for you to adjust your preventer medicine to keep the asthma in control than to rely on a nebuliser to treat acute attacks.

Nevertheless, there is a small minority of patients who may need to have a nebuliser to use at home, but this should only be under the supervision of a specialist or for short periods of time when the nebuliser is on loan from the GP. Elderly people with chronic asthma may be prescribed a nebuliser to use at home to deliver their maintenance medicine.

General Practitioners cannot prescribe nebulisers on the NHS, but a hospital consultant can. There are strict guidelines for doctors on who should and should not have nebulisers for home use. Sometimes people can arrange to borrow a nebuliser from a hospital on a long-term basis.

NB: *If you are thinking of buying a nebuliser, please do not do so without discussing it fully with your GP or specialist first. It may not be the right option for you.*

If you do have a nebuliser at home, please make sure that it is set up correctly and you know exactly how it works. Your doctor or the practice nurse at the surgery should be able to help you do this. You should also know how to keep it clean and when and how often it should be serviced. Also ensure that you know exactly how much of the drug you need to put in the nebuliser and when to take it. Write these instructions

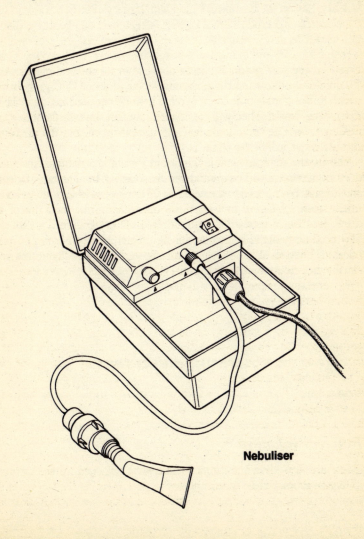

Nebuliser

out clearly and keep them somewhere you can find them easily, even when you are feeling breathless and panicky.

You should also know what to do after you have used the nebuliser to treat a severe attack. Why did the attack occur? Have you let the management plan slide a little? Or is there some other reason for a deterioration in the condition?

NB: *Most people need to see their GP after an acute episode that they have treated themselves.*

Chloro-Fluoro Carbon-Free Inhalers. Since it has been shown that CFCs have the potential to damage the ozone layer, the manufacture of aerosols that contain CFCs is gradually being phased out. From January 1995 in the European Union and January 1996 in the rest of the developed world production of CFCs has been banned except for essential uses. Alternative propellants have been produced for non-medical aerosols but CFC use in medical aerosols has been considered essential. However, they are gradually being phased out for medical use as well. The pharmaceutical industry has developed new non-CFC propellants which do not damage the ozone layer. These new propellants have been extensively tested. They will contain exactly the same medicines as the CFC aerosols. They may look, feel and taste different but the medicine they dispense will be the same.

During the changeover it is important for asthma patients and their doctors or nurses to understand the reasons for the change. Patients should only be changed to the new non-CFC inhalers when they feel confident about changing and after full discussion with their doctor or nurse. It is then important to ensure that future prescriptions are for the new product to avoid confusion during the period when both CFC and non-CFC inhalers are available. If you are at all worried about this you can contact the Asthma Helpline on 0345 01 0203 (charged as a local rate call) from 9am to 9pm Monday to Friday.

· *Asthma medicines* ·

Here is a list of some of the most commonly used medicines in the treatment of asthma.

Reliever inhalers

These are also known as bronchodilators. They open up the airways giving temporary relief of symptoms.

Quick-acting reliever inhalers

GENERIC NAME: *Salbutamol*
TRADE NAMES: *Ventolin, Aerolin autohaler, Maxivent, Salamol, Asmaven, Salbulin.*
AVAILABLE AS: metered-dose inhaler with or without a spacer. Diskhaler, nebuliser, Rotahaler (dry powder), Cyclohaler (dry powder).
ACTION: Works in five to fifteen minutes and lasts approximately four hours.

GENERIC NAME: *Terbutaline Sulphate*
TRADE NAME: *Bricanyl*
AVAILABLE AS: metered dose inhaler with or without spacer, Turbohaler (dry powder), nebuliser.
ACTION: Works in five to fifteen minutes and lasts approximately four hours.

Longer-acting reliever inhalers

GENERIC NAME: *Ipratropium Bromide*
TRADE NAMES: *Atrovent, Atrovent Forte.*
AVAILABLE AS: metered-dose inhaler with or without spacer, Autohaler, nebuliser.
ACTION: works in approximately 40 minutes and lasts approximately six hours.

GENERIC NAME: *Oxitropium Bromide*
TRADE NAME: *Oxivent*
AVAILABLE AS: metered-dose inhaler with or without spacer, Autohaler.
ACTION: works in approximately 40 minutes and lasts approximately six hours.

Long-lasting, slow-acting reliever inhaler

GENERIC NAME: *Salmeterol*
TRADE NAME: *Serevent*
AVAILABLE AS: metered-dose inhaler with or without spacer, Diskhaler.
ACTION: works slowly and lasts for 12 hours approximately.

Non-inhaler relievers

These reliever preparations all work less quickly than the inhaled relievers. None of these treat the inflammation in the airways.

GENERIC NAME: *Theophylline*
TRADE NAMES: *Nuelin, Nuelin SA, Lasma, Slo-phyllin, Theo- dur, Uniphyllin Continus.*
AVAILABLE AS: Tablet, liquid or injection.

GENERIC NAME: *Aminophylline*
TRADE NAMES: *Pecram, Phyllocontin continus, Amnivent.*
AVAILABLE AS: Tablet, injection.

GENERIC NAME: *Salbutamol*
TRADE NAME: *Ventolin*
AVAILABLE AS: Tablet (*Volmax*), Syrup (*Ventolin*), injection.

GENERIC NAME: *Terbutaline Sulphate*
AVAILABLE AS: Tablet (*Bricanyl, Bricanyl SA*), Syrup (Monovent), injection.

GENERIC NAME: *Bambuterol Hydrochloride*
TRADE NAME: *Bambec*
AVAILABLE AS: Tablets.

Preventer inhalers

These medicines treat the inflammation in the airways to prevent asthma symptoms. They need to be taken every day if they are going to work.

Steroid anti-inflammatory preventers

GENERIC NAME: *Beclamethasone Dipropionate*
TRADE NAMES: *Aerobec, Aerobec Forte, Autohaler, Becodisk, Becotide, Beclazone, Filair, Filair Forte, Becotide Rota-cap, Becloforte.*
AVAILABLE AS: metered-dose inhaler with or without spacer, Autohaler, Diskhaler (dry powder), Rotahaler (dry powder).
ACTION: Can take two weeks to have the desired effect.

GENERIC NAME: *Budesonide*
TRADE NAME: *Pulmicort*
AVAILABLE AS: metered-dose inhaler with or without spacer, Turbohaler (dry powder), Nebuhaler.
ACTION: Can take two weeks to have the desired effect.

GENERIC NAME: *Fluticasone Propionate*
TRADE NAME: *Flixotide*
AVAILABLE AS: metered-dose inhaler with or without spacer, Diskhaler (dry powder).
ACTION: Can take two weeks to have the desired effect.

Non-Steroid anti-inflammatory preventers

GENERIC NAME: *Sodium Cromoglycate*
TRADE NAMES: *Intal, Cromogen*
AVAILABLE AS: metered-dose inhaler with or without spacer, Spinhaler (dry powder)
ACTION: Can take six weeks to have the desired effect.

GENERIC NAME: *Nedocromil Sodium*
TRADE NAME: *Tilade*
AVAILABLE AS: metered-dose inhaler
ACTION: Can take six weeks to have the desired effect.

Steroid tablets

Steroid tablets are usually used in short courses of three to fourteen days when asthma is severe and/or out of control. They treat the inflammation in the airways. Sometimes they are used continuously but only by people with severe symptoms that cannot be relieved by inhaled steroids.

NAME: *Prednisolone*
AVAILABLE AS: Tablets, soluble tablets.
ACTION: Takes approximately eight hours to start working.

Compound inhaler preparations

These inhalers, which are a mixture of more than one type of drug are no longer generally recommended, but some people still find them useful. If you are on any of these, ask your doctor about it at your next visit.

Combivent: a mixture of *ipratropium* and *salbutamol*.
Duovent: a mixture of *ipratropium* and *fenoterol*.
Ventide: a mixture of *beclamethasone* and *salbutamol*.
Aerocrom: a mixture of *cromoglycate* and *salbutamol*.

3

PERSONAL MANAGEMENT PLAN

Self-management is becoming a key concept in the treatment of most chronic conditions. Asthma is undoubtedly one of the most important illnesses where this current thinking applies. Self-management is not a 'do-it-yourself and don't let's bother the doctor' routine. Quite the contrary. What it means is that with the help of your doctor or nurse you get to know the condition, as it affects you, recognise the signs of deterioration and take steps to bring it back under control.

Sometimes this will mean contacting the doctor but more often than not you will be able to handle the flare-up yourself. There may be times that you will experience a sudden severe attack in spite of the monitoring and control, but unless you suffer from an acute form of asthma, these occasions should be rare. The aim of self-management is that you should lead the life you want, doing the things you enjoy without asthma getting in the way. For most people with asthma this is very possible.

So what do you do? The previous chapter has listed all the drugs that are used to treat asthma. If you've read the chapter you will have a basic knowledge of what the drugs do. You now know the different function of relievers and preventers and can use them accordingly. When you read the chapter on triggers you will get a pretty good idea of the things in the home, garden or other environment that are likely to aggravate the condition. Hopefully, armed with this information you will be able to avoid some of them. What remains now is to get a handle on your own asthma. When is it good? When is it bad? And how do you recognise when good is getting bad?

There are two ways of recognising a deterioration in the condition. One is by being aware of the symptoms: are you breathless, tight-chested, wheezing or coughing – particularly at night? Are you using your reliever more often? And are you doing less in terms of work, social activities or exercise? All these are signs that the asthma is beginning to slip out of control and you need to look at ways to counteract this. It may be that you need to step up the preventer drug, if you are on one, or go and see the doctor, to be prescribed one perhaps, if you are not. It may be that you need a short course of steroid tablets to bring the condition under control.

The point is that you know something is going wrong and you need to tackle it the right way. In these circumstances many people increase the use of their reliever drug. This, as has been said before, is definitely **not** the answer. It is not the job of reliever medicines to bring the asthma under control – they are there to open the airways.

NB: *If you find that you need to use the relievers more than every four hours, you are in trouble and you must seek medical attention straight-away.*

However, with a good self-management plan you are not going to let things get to this stage.

The second method of monitoring the condition is by means of one of the most important tools in the asthma kit. This is a peak-flow meter. In the UK your doctor can prescribe one for you to use at home and if your asthma is more than mild, it should be an extremely powerful ally in your fight against the illness.

A **Peak-flow meter** is something that measures how fast you can blow out. When you are well, your airways will be open and your breathing good, so your peak-flow measurement will be normal. When your airways have narrowed in response to a trigger the peak-flow reading is likely to drop. What action you take will depend on the range between your best and worst readings. Obviously these are extreme measurements we are talking about. Most of the time you will assess your peak-flow in terms of higher as opposed to lower. This measurement changes during the course of the day. In the afternoons you tend to have a higher reading than you do first thing in the morning. Asthma is usually at its worst very early in the morning.

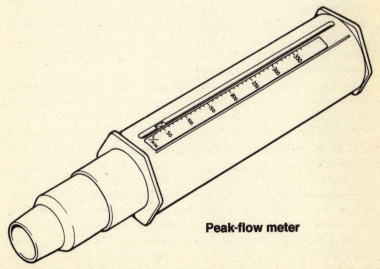

Peak-flow meter

· *Diagnosing* ·

Doctors and asthma nurses use peak-flow meters as a diagnostic tool. If they suspect you have asthma because of your presenting symptoms, they will ask you to blow into a peak-flow meter and take a reading. They may then administer a reliever treatment and take another reading. If the peak-flow measurement has risen more than 10 – 15 per cent above the previous reading it is likely that you have asthma. Alternatively, you may be asked to keep a peak-flow diary. This means blowing into a meter morning and night and charting your readings. Or the doctor or nurse may do an exercise test to see if a narrowing of the airways – and consequent symptoms – happens after exercise. If exercise does reduce the peak-flow and induce symptoms, and the reliever eases them it is also likely that you have asthma.

The health professional will be looking for the following on your peak-flow chart.

- Are the readings within the range for your age and height?
- Are some readings better than others?/Is there a dip some time in the day?
- Are the variations in the readings more than 15 per cent?

What is most significant is the variation in the readings and if there is a dip. Most people find that their reading quite often dips in the morning. But a regular drop in the evening is equally significant.

Peak-flow measurements differ according to age, height and sex. With children it only goes on height and in children under the age of six (or thereabouts) peak-flow meters are not useful.

However, peak-flow readings are very individual. As a rule of thumb it is thought that if you score 80 per cent or over of your best reading your asthma is under control. If you score 60 – 50 per cent or less the condition is serious. But this is a generalisation.

It is far more significant to find out **your own normal reading.** Once you know that you can start recognising when it is low and when it is very low. This is why doctors and asthma nurses prefer to work out target peak-flow readings on an individual basis. Not only do readings differ but the significance of the variation can also be different from person to person.

Suppose, for instance, that there are two women patients who both have a normal peak-flow reading of 400 litres per minute. The self-management plan for the first woman may include a series of actions that need to be taken if it drops below 300 and then 250, and her asthma may be such that she would only call an ambulance if her peak-flow reading dropped to around the 100 mark. With the second patient it may be that she will need urgent medical attention when her peak-flow goes to 250 litres per minute because at that stage she is actually quite ill.

So some people can function quite happily when their peak-flow is at 80 per cent of normal while others will need medical attention at that stage.

Doctors have two ways of diagnosing asthma. If the condition improves after the patient has been on the anti-asthma drugs, this is an indication of asthma. But of course this improvement can take several weeks, if not months, to be noticed. The second is with a peak-flow meter. If after the patient has been taking medication the peak-flow readings show an improvement in the three pointers mentioned above, the diagnosis of asthma is confirmed.

· *Self-managing* ·

First and foremost you should work out with your doctor or asthma nurse a series of steps to take to manage the condition. Step one will be the normal routine where, for example, you use your preventer inhaler twice a day and your reliever as and when necessary but no more than four times a day. If you start getting symptoms or your peak-flow reading shows a deterioration you then go on to step two in the management plan worked out with your health professional. This may mean increasing the dose of your inhaled preventer. How much you increase it by and for how long is something else you will need to have planned. At this stage you are very likely to have got your asthma under control, but if you haven't you will move on to step three. This may mean taking steroid tablets or calling the doctor or ambulance or both. Again, you will have planned beforehand what you do under these circumstances.

The point is that this self-management plan should be tailor-made for you and aimed to cope with the condition according to the level of severity currently being presented. However, there are guidelines which have been produced to standardize the treatment of asthma, both in the doctor's surgery and in hospitals. In Chapter 6 I give you a very much abbreviated version of the step-by-step guide that may be used by your doctor or asthma nurse.

Armed with a peak-flow meter and a chart you can be your own lay-physician by assessing the state of your condition daily and taking the necessary action when you observe a deterioration. It is important to note your best reading because it is a useful barometer of how good or bad your condition is at any given time.

To do this you need to blow into a peak-flow meter morning and night. Try and get into a routine of doing it at approximately the same time each day whenever possible. But don't be obsessional about the timing. **It is much better to do it regularly every day rather than worry about getting the time right.**

Here are guidelines on how to use a peak-flow meter as described by the National Asthma Campaign:

- Check that the marker (pointer) on the meter is at zero.
- Sit upright or stand.
- Hold the meter level (flat), and keep your fingers away from the pointer.
- Take a big breath in.
- Close your lips firmly around the mouthpiece.
- Blow out as hard and as quickly as you can.
- Look at your score.
- Reset the marker and start again.
- Do this three times and write the best score on your chart.

Charts are available from your doctor, nurse or from the Family Health Service Authority in booklet form (*Form FP1010*).

These charts are not difficult to use and they really can show you, quite graphically, the state of your asthma at any given time. Look at the three charts I have given you: notice that I have underlined the point at which the reading is 80 per cent of best and where it is 60 per cent of best. You may find this helpful to do yourself. Some doctors and nurses will mark levels on your charts for you. The three charts illustrated are based on the best of three blows on the peak-flow meter and are of a person whose best result on the peak-flow meter is 450 litres per minute.

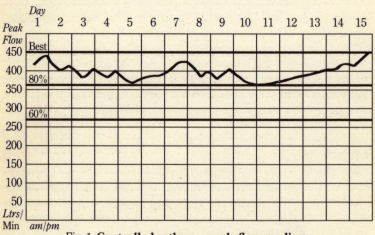

Fig. 1 **Controlled asthma – peak-flow readings**

Fig. 1 shows that the patient's asthma is under control. It never dips below 80 per cent of best and when it touches the 80 per cent level it starts to rise again – presumably because the patient has been alerted and taken action.

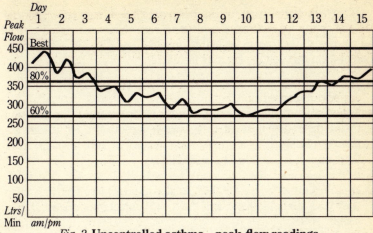

Fig. 2 Uncontrolled asthma – peak-flow readings

Fig. 2 shows a much more varied pattern with highs and lows showing that the asthma is not being controlled. On Days 8, 10 and 11 the condition is quite serious, but again, our patient has handled the situation and from day 12 things are looking a lot better and the asthma is getting back under control.

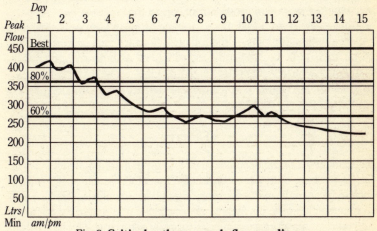

Fig. 3 Critical asthma – peak-flow readings

Fig. 3 chart shows that the person is in trouble and needs to get urgent medical attention. At Day 4 they should have started getting worried and taking action. Days 7 and 8 are pretty serious and whatever treatment is being taken, it is clearly not good enough because by day 11 the deterioration looks set to continue. Ideally on day 7 when the breathing had got below 60 per cent of best, the patient should have sought medical help. Now they need it urgently!

What action you need to take when your recordings show that the asthma is out of control is something that must be worked out in advance with your doctor or asthma nurse. The following is an indication of what this action plan may include.

- At the first signs of a deterioration in the condition double your dose of **preventer** medicine.
- Note how many days it takes for the condition to settle down and keep taking the double dose after the asthma is controlled for at least the number of days it took you to bring about that improvement. After that you can go back to your normal dose.
- If the increased dose of preventer medicine has not noticeably improved the asthma go to the next step of your plan. This may be to start your steroid tablets. Or it maybe to contact your doctor. It may include both.
- *If you are having problems in breathing and are using your reliever every four hours but if the effects of the reliever are not lasting for four hours, you are in trouble – get medical help without delay!*

In any event please remember that if you have an attack which has required emergency treatment, whether this has been self-managed or you have had to go to hospital, you need to see your doctor to follow it up. It may be that you need to revise your self-management plan to try and avoid these kind of attacks from happening.

It must also be said that there are some people whose peak-flow does not drop with symptoms. Although peak-flow is a very important diagnostic tool, it is not the only indication of asthma by any means. Symptoms are a very important sign that all is not well. If you have persistent asthma symptoms you must take notice even if your peak-flow is registering reasonable levels.

· DAVID ·

David makes training documentaries and promotional films which often entails working outdoors in all kinds of weather. Much of his work is done in front of the camera, presenting the documentaries. He also does voice-overs. Keeping his asthma under control is essential for his work. As you read his story you will see that his worst attack came when he did not take the asthma symptoms seriously. Now his condition is very much under control.

As I child I had a very bad chest. I don't think asthma was diagnosed so often then. My condition was described as 'a wheezy chest'. I had an awful lot of time off junior school. It got to the stage where my grandmother gave me a shilling every time I could make it to school for a whole week without having a day off. I didn't pick up many shillings!

It then seemed to clear and unless I did something like cross-country running, which wasn't very good because of the combination of cold air and exercise, it never really bothered me as a teenager or in my twenties. I knew there were things I should avoid doing, like running for the bus, which made me wheezy, but apart from that I didn't get attacks out of the blue for random reasons.

When I was in my thirties it came back again and I started to get a little bit wheezy for no apparent reason. That was when I was first prescribed Ventolin. But I hardly used it in the early days. Then it gradually got worse and worse until I had a bad attack four or five years ago.

If ever I got a cold it would always affect my chest. The streaming nose was the easy bit for me, because what followed was weeks of wheezy coughing with congested lungs. That was what happened in this case. I was working hard and there was no chance of taking time off. I was supposed to be filming that week. I work freelance and if you don't work you don't get paid. I kept going but I was gradually getting weaker and weaker and my chest was getting worse and worse. In the end I had to give in and just lie in bed. If I got out of bed I was so breathless that I couldn't do anything other than lie there. That was how I kept the symptoms at bay. The interesting thing is that I didn't regard it as that serious. Asthma was seen to be something that was partly self-induced. The feeling was that it was your own fault in the first place and secondly you would get over it. There was no need to take anything. The impression was that if you kept still and calmed down you'd recover. But I didn't. I got progressively worse.

The doctor did come at one point but the only useful thing he did was to tell me that if I got any worse I was to go straight into hospital. I was taking Ventolin more and more frequently. Every time I felt worse I'd take another puff of Ventolin. I felt guilty about doing it because it was like admitting that I wasn't well. I felt that the less I could take the Ventolin the better but I had to keep taking it to keep going. But it got to the stage when even the Ventolin wasn't strong enough and I was taken into hospital and given the full treatment – the nebulisers, oral steroids and all the rest of it.

Since then there's been a total change in the way in which I regard my asthma. I take inhaled steroids every day. It keeps the inflammation down so I hardly have to use the reliever at all. I still carry it around just in case but I rarely use it. If I get a cold now I up the dose of inhaled steroid a bit which stops it going on to my chest. That's the big advantage of taking the inhaled steroid. It keeps the symptoms at bay.

Now I get a cold like everybody else. Two days of a streaming nose and a blocked-up feeling but nothing goes on to my chest.

The big eye-opener for me was finding out that if you didn't treat the asthma it actually damaged your lungs. The amount of inflammation that you were allowing to continue in your lungs was damaging the lung tissue. Therefore you were silly not to treat it. It was better treated even if it meant taking something all the time. I think that was the mental shift. Before I used to feel that basically I was like everybody else but I just had this weak chest and I had to avoid doing certain things. Now I've accepted that it is more of *a long term condition that I'm always going to have. It may get worse or better but I've got to keep doing something about it to avoid damaging my lungs any further.*

I am a video presenter. I stand in front of the camera and yap into it. This often involves filming in cold and windy places when you don't feel great and it entails a lot of standing around. Standing in front of a camera is a fairly stressful thing. Before I was on the inhaled steroid I seemed to have the symptoms more often and they seemed to come on for no particular reason. I always had a reliever inhaler with me and I was always using it to keep the symptoms at bay. But it wasn't controlling the asthma like the inhaler steroid does.

If I had to go into town to do a voice-over I'd go out from a warm house to a cold street and run to a tube station. The cold air and the running would make me quite wheezy. There's nothing like going in front of a highly sensitive microphone and trying to read a script for people to realise that you are wheezy. It then takes longer to do the script. If you overrun the time you don't get booked again because you're more expensive. Inevitably I was taking puffs of blue reliever before I'd do a session. Also you don't want people to see you taking puffs of your inhaler because they may think they've hired a lame duck.

But all that's gone now. The inhaled steroid has been very successful. Asthma doesn't affect my working life at all. Now there are very few things that bring on the symptoms and the symptoms are mild and easy to treat.

· JEFFREY ·

Jeffrey is a 21-year-old student reading maths at Warwick University. His first asthma attack came out of the blue at the age of 14 and he believes that he is likely to have the condition for the rest of his life. However, in addition to his studies, Jeffrey is a keen dancer entering competitions for ballroom and Latin dancing. As long as he keeps his asthma under control it does not inhibit his demanding life-style. He does this by taking daily peak-flow readings and adjusting his medication accordingly. Here is his story:

I was walking to school one morning when I started to have breathing problems. It was quite a cold winter's day and by the time I got to school I found I just could not catch my breath. I was doing GCSE Dance at the time and I had to sit out.

For the next two months I was constantly breathless and every now and again the breathing difficulty would get quite severe. The doctors kept telling me that I had a cold or a chest infection. But it was nothing of the sort. Eventually I had a bad attack and landed up in hospital. The specialist there diagnosed asthma.

I have since agreed a plan with my hospital doctor which is based on my peak-flow readings. I take these night and morning. My normal peak-flow reading is somewhere between 650 to 700 litres per minute and my usual medication is two puffs of Serevent and four puffs of Pulmicort night and morning. These are taken through a spacer. If my peak-flow drops to 500 I have to double the dose of Pulmicort. I don't take extra Serevent because more than a certain amount of it starts me shaking. If it drops to below about 330 I have some steroid tablets which I'm supposed to take. If it continues to drop after that I know I have to call an ambulance.

I've only had to phone for an ambulance once. That was last year when I was living in the Halls of Residence at University. I think the attack was triggered by a mixture of different things. I was under quite a bit of stress with exams and assessments and the weather was hot with a high pollen count. Pollen at that time was a big trigger for me as I also suffer from hay fever. On top of all this there was a different lady cleaning my room and I think she sprayed something in the room that I reacted to.

I was doing my peak-flow readings and I could see that they were getting low. I went through the steps, taking the doubled dose of Pulmicort. But at that time I didn't have the steroid tablets. When my reading got towards the 300 mark I knew I had to call an ambulance but I could not breathe well enough to make the phone call. I had to get the warden who was on duty to phone for one. He kept me calm in his room while the ambulance came. They took me off to hospital where they brought the attack under control. Since then my action plan has included the oral steroids but so far I haven't had to take them.

I find the worst part of an attack is the fear. Sometimes you feel that you are not going to get your breath at all. That really frightens me at times.

Having asthma doesn't affect my life. A few people will tell me that I can't do things because I have asthma and I find that very annoying. My dance teacher told me at one point that she would not teach me the fast dances like the jive and the cha-cha. She said I couldn't do them because of my asthma and she'd only teach me the slow dances. So I promptly got up and did a remarkably fast cha-cha. I think I proved her wrong.

I have been dancing since I was three years old. It is part of my life. I usually take a dose of reliever treatment before I go on the floor and I very seldom get out of breath. Occasionally if they put the jive on too fast I will be breathless coming off the floor but it's not that much of a problem. Give me a couple of minutes to sit down and I'm usually okay. If I feel bad I'll take a puff of Bricanyl but that doesn't happen too often.

I know quite a few asthmatics who dance. Asthma doesn't stop any of us.

As long as I keep it under control the asthma doesn't affect me. I spend some minutes night and morning doing the peak-flow and taking the medication but that usually sees me all right for the rest of the day and I can do what I want.

The only thing that is a bit of a problem is anaesthetics. I had a stiff toe joint and recently had to have an operation to free it. This entailed breaking the toe which was quite painful. They gave me the anaesthetic and I went out all right. They did the operation and I was back in the ward but as I was coming round I discovered I could not breathe. They didn't have the right medication on the ward to give me apart from oxygen which worked eventually. But it was quite scary for a few minutes.

Most of my friends know I have asthma and can cope with it. It's in my family, along with eczema and hay fever, but I seem to be the one who is the worst affected. It is surprising how many people have asthma or know someone who has it. Most people tend to take it in their stride.

I've been told that since it came on so late, I've probably got asthma for the rest of my life. But so long as I can keep it under control I'm not particularly bothered about that.

4

EMERGENCIES

The best thing you can do about emergency treatment is to try and avoid it. So one of the aims of this book is to help you to recognise when an asthma attack is brewing and to take action so that it doesn't happen. In the past it was thought that attacks happened out of the blue. Now with the use of peak-flow meters it is seen that people generally start to deteriorate over a period of time – maybe two weeks or so – before there is a sudden worsening. What seems like a sudden attack may, in fact, not be one.

If you are aware of your symptoms and recognise when they are getting worse you can start taking steps which can, in most cases, avoid an acute attack. What action you take depends on the plan you have worked out with your doctor or asthma nurse as has already been explained in Chapter 3.

However, with the best will in the world, no one can guarantee that they will never get an acute attack or need emergency treatment. For people with the rarer brittle asthma these attacks come suddenly even if they have been careful to keep up their management routine. The point is, how do you recognise when an attack requires emergency treatment and how do you handle the situation? These are the issues discussed in this chapter.

For every individual asthma is a different illness. In the same way as the things that trigger your attacks are not necessarily the same as those that set off someone else's, the nature of your attacks is not likely to be identical to that of other asthma patients. Knowing asthma as it affects you, or if you are the parent of an asthma sufferer, understanding the condition as it occurs in your child, is of paramount importance. If you can recognise through symptoms or peak-flow readings that the condition needs extra attention, you will have come a long way in managing your asthma.

It is also important to talk to your GP or asthma nurse and get some guidelines as to what might be the hazard warnings in your condition. Part of your self-management plan must include what you do in an emergency. After you have been through the steps, at what stage do you call for help? Exactly what you do in an acute attack is something that you must understand and be familiar with and feel confident about carrying out. To give you a very general idea, here are some points you might like to bear in mind.

First of all learn to recognise the signs that herald an attack. These 'prodomal' symptoms differ from person to person. If you can learn to recognise your own, you can prepare yourself for what is about to follow. Here are some examples:

- Itchy skin.
- Itchy nose.
- Sickness.
- Light-headedness.
- Shortness of breath over and above the usual.
- You experience symptoms more often than usual.
- You experience symptoms at night.

In addition there may be other signs:

- A descending pattern in your peak-flow readings.
- A larger than usual variation in readings from morning to evening.
- **You are using your reliever treatment more often – and especially if it is more than every four hours.**

This last pointer is the most important one. At this stage take an extra dose of your reliever treatment. Wait five or 10 minutes and if there is no improvement take the reliever again. If the reliever doesn't help, take the situation very seriously.

NB: *Remember that the reliever puffer is blue.*

The most important sign of an attack is when your reliever drug is not rescuing you from your breathing difficulties. Never ignore this warning. It means that you cannot handle the situation on your own and you need medical help.

Whether this help should be sought by ringing the doctor or calling for an ambulance is something you should work out in advance with your GP. Most of the time your doctor should be able to treat the attack. Please do not be afraid to contact him or her and don't leave it to the last minute. It is known that most of the bad asthma attacks happen in the early hours of the morning, so phoning the doctor at this time is not an unusual step for an asthma patient. All doctors arrange for round-the-clock medical cover for their patients.

However, if you are worried, if the attack has deteriorated suddenly, or if you've already agreed this plan of action with your doctor – call an ambulance. Tell them that you are having an asthma attack so that they know to send a supply of oxygen and a nebulizer in the ambulance.

NB: Please tell anyone you live or work with, or are likely to be with at a time of an asthma attack, that if they call an ambulance they need to ensure that the ambulance is carrying the correct equipment.

While you are waiting for the doctor or ambulance to arrive, continue to give yourself treatment even though the reliever may not seem to be working. You will need to step up the reliever treatment and ideally you should have discussed the dose with your doctor. What is often suggested is one puff every 10 seconds. Please note that this kind of dosage is only permissible for emergency treatment.

If you have a spacer, use that taking one puff every 15 seconds. If you do not have a spacer but there is someone around who can make you an emergency one as described in Chapter 2, ask them to do so.

Sit in a position that is comfortable for you and try your best to relax. Most people feel more comfortable sitting up. If you sit up or sit forward it will aid lung expansion and you should feel a bit better.

Some people like to sit near an open window because they feel better that way and less panicky. Remember, help is on the way.

Try and slow your breathing down as best you can. Not only will this help you relax but it will also save your energy.

· *Silent chest* ·

Although wheezing and coughing are known symptoms of asthma, they are not always present with the condition. Some people do not wheeze at all. However, this 'silent' type of asthma is not a good sign. Quite the contrary, it may be an indication that airways are very narrow and little air is moving in and out. Your breathing may be silent but you need urgent medical attention. If you don't get it your breathing may get so bad that not only will you have difficulty in breathing and speaking, but as less and less oxygen gets into the bloodstream, your lips will turn blue and the next step will be that you lose consciousness.

NB: *The sentence above describes a very severe and life threatening attack and is very unusual.*

· *Chest X-rays* ·

Chest X-rays are done on some people who come into casualty. If the patient has very suddenly gone breathless it may be that one of their lungs has collapsed. This is a rare occurrence. Most people coming into casualty who present the usual symptoms and tell a normal asthma story are offered chest X-rays routinely. But in childhood cases the medics on duty would only do a chest X-ray if something sounded strange.

Suppose, for instance, that the lung has collapsed, giving the patient medicine to open their airways isn't going to be any good, and they may need different treatment. So doctors have to bear it in mind if they suspect that the symptoms are something other than asthma. You can't see asthma on an X-ray.

A seven-year-old who is brought into casualty with the symptoms and an account that sounds like someone suffering with straightforward asthma, is not going to be offered a chest X-ray. A 60-year-old who has been working, for example, in an asbestos factory, smoked all his life and has a cough or is wheezy, is very likely to be offered an X-ray because the chances are that the problem may be something other than asthma, or that something else may be complicating the asthma. Doctors have to investigate the other possibilities if only to rule them out.

· *Blood tests* ·

Sometimes patients need to have a blood test to measure the amount of oxygen there is in the blood. Sometimes it can be uncomfortable or, on occasions, a painful experience. This is because unlike most blood tests where the blood is taken from a vein, in this case the blood is taken from an artery. It is a difficult test to do. Unfortunately since it is so uncomfortable, it puts many people off going to hospital for emergency treatment for their asthma – just in case they get this blood test again!

One of the reasons for doing it is that some people come in collapsed, unable to speak and seriously ill. It is important to see how much oxygen there is in the blood and how much carbon dioxide (the exhaust gas you normally breathe out) is building up. According to these figures the medical team may or may not want to take the patient straight to the intensive care unit and assist his or her ventilation. Assessing the case can be a real advantage at this stage because that's when you get a true reading. Once the patient has been given oxygen and inhaler treatment the reading will show plenty of oxygen in the blood: then staff will not be able to gauge accurately what the situation was before the oxygen was administered. So the medical team want to do the oxygen test very quickly as soon as the patient is brought it.

· *Casualty* ·

People coming into casualty with acute severe asthma may seem to be surrounded by staff and equipment very quickly, depending on how serious they are. They may have their blood pressure checked. They may be put on to a machine to test the oxygen in the blood which involves wearing a clip on a finger or toe. Blood may also be taken. They may or may not need a nebuliser. This is team work. The casualty nurses will be taking observations and getting the nebuliser and oxygen ready and possibly asking questions all at the same time, while someone else is taking the blood. The patient may well be given steroid tablets to treat the inflammation. If they can swallow, these will be given in the form of tablets: if they can't, they will be given as an injection.

Accident and Emergency staff in hospitals are very well versed in treating acute attacks. But as a rule they are not there to investigate the whys and wherefores of the attack or to offer you follow-up treatment. In treatment terms they are the relievers, if you like. If you want to treat the condition you need to consult the preventers who come in the shape of your doctor or asthma nurse. If you've been treated in hospital for an attack you must see your GP or asthma nurse, even if you are not a new asthma patient. You need to discuss your self-management plan with a view to adjusting the treatment so that an acute attack doesn't happen again.

TRIGGERS

Avoiding the things that trigger asthma, if and when you can, is obviously worth considering. This is easier said than done but it must also be said that for most people avoidance can, to some extent, be achieved. Virtually everyone who has asthma has some kind of allergy. Allergies are a significant trigger. If you can identify the things that trigger your asthma and if you can avoid some of them, even some of the time, this will be an important part of your asthma management plan. It is very unlikely that avoidance of triggers will obviate treatment, but you may be able to cut down on the frequency and severity of the condition in this way.

It must also be said that you do have to balance quality of life with trigger avoidance. Shutting yourself away in case you come across something that might trigger your asthma is not a way to live. Happiness is a good antidote to most negative situations. So let this chapter be a guide as to the kind of things that might affect your asthma. If you can avoid any of them without curtailing your activities then try and do so. But be aware that there are bound to be triggers that you cannot avoid and you shouldn't worry about it.

Writing in *Low Allergen Living* produced by the National Asthma Campaign, Dr Martyn Partridge says: 'Many things may narrow the airways in asthma, for example, exercise, cold air, exhaust fumes, cigarette smoke, aerosol sprays, chemicals and strong smells.

'While at high concentrations some chemicals will affect normal airways, the airways of asthmatics are hyper-reactive. This means that the airways narrow with fewer stimuli or smaller doses of stimuli than are required to narrow normal airways. It is now appreciated that allergy underlies the development of this hyper-reactivity in 80–90 per cent of children and 50–60 per cent of adults with asthma by causing inflammation in the airways. The major allergens which contribute to the asthmatic state and induce a chronic inflammation within the airways in asthma are now recognised to be indoor allergens related to house dust mites and to household pets. The allergens generated by these animals are airborne and are breathed in; they seem to be more important for the exacerbation of asthma than substances that are eaten.' Dr Partridge is a consultant chest physician with a special interest in asthma.

The difficulty is that what triggers asthma may differ from person to person. Furthermore, it is very unlikely that it is a single trigger that is causing the problem. It is usually a cocktail of allergens that aggravate the condition. However, as Dr Partridge says there are some that are known to trigger asthma in a large proportion of patients and it is these which this chapter examines.

Eradicating or avoiding some of the allergens in your environment is time-consuming and irritating, but it is worth a genuine try. It is very unlikely that you will be able to avoid all the allergens in your life, but cutting down on them may pay dividends in terms of your health. Your asthma should improve and you may be able to reduce the amount of medication you use. And that has to be a bonus. As has been said before, drugs are an important ally in the treatment of asthma. The best drug treatment is the one that uses the minimum of medication to achieve the desired effect. You can do this by taking a dedicated look at how to minimise the triggers in your life and in so doing take another step towards controlling the asthma.

There was a time when people used desensitisation treatments to reduce allergic reactions, but in Britain this is not thought to be safe or particularly helpful for asthma these days. As ever, the best way is the hard way, so let's look at some of the known triggers and examine, where possible, how best to avoid them.

· Smoking ·

Active Smoking

Numerous studies have shown the deleterious affects of smoking. It kills thousands more people a year than road accidents and in this country alone accounts for some 100,000 premature deaths a year through lung and heart disease. There is no doubt that people with asthma are particularly sensitive to the air they breathe and the pollutants therein – yet we know that some 20 per cent of asthma sufferers smoke.

Asthma is a condition that affects the air passages of the lungs. These airways narrow and become twitchy when an irritant is breathed in. Cigarette smoke is high on the list of irritants. Often the airways of a person with asthma vary daily, being narrow one day and normal the next. A smoker's airways suffer damage and these often remain narrow making the condition chronic – unless, of course, the smoker gives up the habit. The good news with smoking and asthma is that the situation is often reversible. Unfortunately, it can take up to 12 months before you see a really good improvement and the condition can seem to have got worse before it gets better.

According to the National Asthma Campaign: 'A study of teenagers with asthma who smoked cigarettes showed they had poorer asthma control and worse lung function by the time they reached their twenties and that their asthma had a tendency to persist. If you have asthma and you smoke, you are increasing the risk of an attack and may be permanently damaging your airways.'

No one is suggesting that it is easy to give up smoking. If you smoke regularly you are likely to be dependent on, if not addicted to, cigarettes. People are dependent on cigarettes for a wide variety of reasons and some of these are linked quite deeply to emotional needs. This is why it is not particularly helpful to issue blanket statements on the best way of giving up smoking. Nicotine patches will work for some people but not others who may prefer to chew gum, see a hypnotherapist, take a course of acupuncture and so on. A good starting point would be to contact *Quitline* (see Useful Addresses, page 149). They will try and find out what smoking means for you: how long you have smoked, how many cigarettes a day, what are the most important cigarettes of the day and so on. They will probably be interested in whether you've tried giving up before and what happened then. The point is that they try and build up a pattern of your smoking and with that help you to decide what is most likely to work for you. In addition, *Quitline* can put you in touch with individual counsellors and support groups throughout the country. They are available from 9am to 5pm Monday to Friday.

Passive Smoking

If you smoke and you have a child with asthma, please bear in mind that the best thing in the world you can do for that child is to give up smoking. It beats expensive holidays, toys, clothes and outings. Children brought up in homes where the parents smoke are much more prone to respiratory diseases – including asthma – than children who live in smoke-free homes. Their lung function and growth is not as good as children whose parents do not smoke. Living in a house where the air is polluted with tobacco smoke will certainly aggravate the condition of an asthma sufferer. Most people put good health as a requirement above and before anything else. This must surely also be the case for a child who has virtually all his life still ahead of him.

Women who smoke during pregnancy increase the risk of their child developing asthma. The foetus of a mother who smokes develops less well in the womb than that of a mother who does not. Babies of mothers who smoke are usually born smaller than those of mothers who don't. Cot deaths have also been linked to passive smoking. Your midwife or health visitor can give you information on this.

Passive smoking is an insidious problem to tackle. A National Asthma Campaign survey has shown that cigarette smoke is capable of causing asthma attacks in 83 per cent of asthma sufferers. Only 15 per cent of the smoke produced by a cigarette is inhaled by the smoker. The rest streams out or is puffed out, and is inhaled by those in the company of the smoker. Fortunately, these days smoking is seen as an anti-social habit and increasingly banned from public places. Do try and avoid venues where smoking is allowed whenever you can. Obviously this is going to be impossible in places like pubs, bars, discos and parties. It would be a shame to miss out on social gatherings of this kind, so if you are planning on being in a smoky atmosphere, make sure you take your reliever with you. It may also be that you will need to step up your pre-venter treatment for a day or two afterwards. In any event, keep an extra watch on your asthma. If your asthma is bad, think again before spending time in a very smoky atmosphere. Unless it is unavoidable, or very important to you, it may not be worth the possible consequences.

In your own home you can be quite tough. You may have friends who smoke and you may feel sensitive about asking them not to smoke in your house. If you live with a smoker that will certainly be a problem. There is a difficulty about asking people not to smoke because, one feels, they have rights. And so they do. Anyone has a right to injure them-selves. But they do not have a right to injure you or your children. Look at it this way. If your friend or partner had the habit of sticking pins in you, there would be no problem in telling him or her to stop. It would be obviously injurious so you would feel justified. You may not be able to see the damage that smoking produces but you know for a fact that it exists. So you don't have to put up with it. Tell the smoker that he (or she) can smoke if he must but he must do it outside in the open air where it is not quite so polluting.

Dealing with tobacco smoke at work is another difficult issue and this is discussed in Chapter 7.

· *House dust mites* ·

These microscopic creatures are related to spiders and ticks. They are about a third of a millimetre long and so are not visible to the naked eye. They are found, in their millions, in every home, no matter how clean. The house dust mite is the single most important allergy provoker in Britain and is implicated in triggering asthma in people who are sensi-tive to the allergen they produce. It is the droppings of these creatures that cause the problem. One of the things produced in these droppings is the allergen *DER PI*.

House dust mites are particularly prolific in damp climates such as ours. They thrive on moist and warm environments and live in mat-tresses, carpets, settees and soft furnishings of all sorts.

House dust mites have a life-span of about six weeks. During this time each female can produce anything up to 80 eggs. It takes between three and four weeks for the eggs to develop into fully-fledged adults. So you can see why they are so numerous and so difficult to eradicate and you certainly will not be able to get rid of them entirely from your house. But here are ways to cut down on their presence.

Furnishing and Bedding

● Carpets are great gatherers of dust, particularly bedroom carpets where the humidity is likely to be higher. So wooden floors, lino or tiles are probably a better bet particularly if they are vacuumed or damp dusted daily. Dispense with rugs or if you must have them, make sure they are small,light, easily washable and wash them often.

● Try and keep furnishing simple and easy to clean. Plain wood or plastic chairs are easier to clean than upholstered ones. Choose curtains or blinds that are easy to wash rather than heavy fabrics. Venetian blinds collect a lot of dust so avoid these. Fabric blinds that you can damp dust are a good idea.

● Textured wallpaper, wall hangings and plants can also collect dust and fungi. Dried flowers, especially, are great dust gatherers and so are books.

● Mattresses are a major home for house dust mites. The warmth and humidity generated by the human body sleeping on a mattress provides cosy conditions for these creatures. Also, the shed skin scales, which the dust mite feeds on, are found in abundance on the upper layers of the mattress. If you are buying a new mattress you may like to know that you can buy one with a special interliner in them which is said to protect against house dust mites and their droppings.

Cover existing mattresses with airtight plastic covers which are available by mail order. Alternatively, you can enclose the mattress in an interliner. Both these methods act as a barrier between you and house dust mites and are away of keeping the dust mite and its droppings at bay. These covers are easy to keep clean. Mail-order houses which supply both methods are advertised quite widely. You do not need to spend a lot of money on mattress covers as the cheaper ones work just as well.

You don't need to cover cot mattresses as most have covers anyway, but it is desirable to have a new mattress for each new baby.

● Bedding should be of man-made and washable fibres rather than natural fibres. This goes for duvets and pillows. Duvets are far preferable to blankets, but if you must use the latter make sure they are cotton cellular ones and wash them at a high temperature every two weeks. Wash sheets and pillowcases and duvets frequently. Wash in temperatures as hot as the fabric washing instructions will allow. Anti-allergy pillows and duvets which you can wash in very hot temperatures are available as are plastic covers or interliners to cover duvets and pillow-cases. But be careful with young children as there is a risk of suffocation from plastic coverings. You can also buy pillows with interliners incorporated into them. If you use these methods you will not need to wash the bedding so frequently. But you will need to wipe plastic covers with a damp cloth.

- Regularly air pillows, duvets and mattresses. Remove all feather bedding and pillows.
- Soft toys are a major living ground for the house dustmite. If your child has asthma try and cut down on the amount of these toys that he or she has if you cannot eliminate them altogether, and try and discourage them from being kept on the bed. If this is not possible, wash the toys every week. You can also put the toys into plastic bags and place in the freezer for five or six hours (or more) and then give them a hot machine wash. If you do this regularly, say once a month, it should keep the dust mite population down.
- Padded headboards should be avoided as they are difficult to keep dust-free.
- Bunk beds for children which asthma should be avoided but if there is no choice the top bunk is preferable for a child with asthma as the dust mite droppings in the mattress above can come through to the person in the bunk below.

Cleaning

Always damp-dust as dry dusting releases the mite droppings into the atmosphere. All surfaces should be damp-dusted at least once a week.

Vacuuming is preferable to sweeping. If you need a new vacuum cleaner get one with the best filtration system you can afford. (You can look at *Which* magazine April 1993 where they have tested filters.) Most vacuum cleaners will retain virtually all the larger dust particles but the sub-microscopic particles leak through the filter system and become airborne until such time as they settle on the furniture. These airborne particles of house dust mite droppings can trigger the asthma. Also, vacuum cleaners become contaminated with the dust they collect and therefore each time you switch on the cleaner, dust particles are released into the room. This is why a good filtration system can be helpful to some extent. But if you don't need a new vacuum cleaner don't buy one as it probably doesn't warrant the extra expenditure.

If you are the person with asthma try not to do the vacuuming. If you really have to don't do it every day. If dust mites really are a problem for you, try wearing a mask when you are vacuuming. Cyclists' masks are all right to use and are widely available.

Incidentally, carpet-washing machines are not thought to be of any help in reducing the house dust mite population. Most leave a small residue of water behind in the carpet pile and this added humidity may in fact encourage these creatures to increase and multiply!

Minimize damp

You can do this by avoiding humidifiers and vaporisers. Repair leaky pipes, defective walls and roofs. Extractor fans in kitchens and bathrooms are also a good investment because they tend to reduce condensation and the latter encourages both house dust mites and moulds. Keeping the air as dry as possible is the best way of keeping dust mites at bay but, having said that, ducted air heating can be a problem because when you switch it on it can blow dust particles around the room.

· Pets ·

It is estimated that about 40 per cent of children who have asthma are allergic to cats. More or less any furry pet can produce an allergic reaction in someone who is sensitised but cats seem to be the worst offenders. Children with asthma can also be allergic to dogs but the figures here are between 10 and 15 per cent.

It is worth knowing that the allergy may not show itself straight away. It often takes time to build up, but a person who is sensitised may start wheezing as soon as they enter a room or house even if the cat is not there at the time. So if someone tells you not to worry because they are going remove the cat from the room, worry anyway, because the allergen will still be there for months despite the banished cat. Pets that are kept in the home shed their dander all over the house so virtually every room is affected.

Whether the cat has short hair or long hair is immaterial. The allergic reaction is caused by dander which are the small scales in the cat's skin. Cats shed dander continuously whether they are of the short-haired or long-haired variety. Cat's urine and dried saliva are also allergenic. (The allergy, by the way, may take the form of eczema as well as asthma.) It can take several weeks or months for the asthma to improve once the cat has gone because it can take that long to get rid of the last traces of the dander.

With dogs the problem is also the dander, so again it makes no difference whether the dog is short-haired or long-haired or whether it is a breed that doesn't shed hair at all. The dog's saliva and urine are again implicated.

Allergic reactions have been reported from many animals, not just dogs and cats. **Birds** may also trigger asthma symptoms and again it is the dander and droppings which seem to cause the allergy rather than the feathers. **Horses** are also very likely to cause sensitivity. In fact even if the rider isn't sensitive, the hair brought in on the clothes of the rider can cause a reaction in someone else in the family who has asthma and is allergic to horses. If this is the case, let the rider ride by all means. But keep the clothes out of the house and wash them somewhere else, in a launderette for instance. **Rabbits, hamsters, guineapigs** and **mice** are also very likely to cause an allergic reaction in someone with asthma.

It does seem a grim picture for anyone who likes animals and feels that pets are an important part of family life. But please bear in mind that the control of moderate-to-severe asthma often entails the use of drugs on a permanent basis and you have to weigh the disadvantages of this against the pleasures of owning a pet.

· *Gardens* ·

Airborne pollens are those which are likely to provoke asthma attacks (or hay fever) in susceptible people. These include all grasses, together with some tree pollens, notably hazels, oaks and birches. Trees, grasses and plants pollinate at different times of the year, but from early April to September gardens can be hazardous for people with asthma. This does not mean that you cannot enjoy the pleasure of a garden, but it does require that you plan your garden around your asthma.

With expert gardening help, the National Asthma Campaign designed a garden which was extremely attractive but at the same time kept the allergy factor to an all-time low. This garden was exhibited at the Chelsea Flower Show in 1994 where it won a Silver Medal.

The garden had no lawns because of the grass factor. In place of lawns were inexpensive terraces with plants in pots. Mowing is the number one gardening hazard for anyone with asthma because it releases the pollen and mould spores into the air which is inhaled causing wheeziness, narrowing of airways and so on. If you do have lawns in your garden it is best to use an electric rollermower.

Hedges were also excluded because they hold vast amounts of dust and pollens. Cutting hedges can release these into the air. Fences are preferable.

Organic mulches including bark and manures were not used as these break down and release mould spores. Gravel mulch which not only retains moisture but also reduces the growth of weeds, was used in preference. Weeding is a task to avoid in the garden and again you can do this by using plants which give ground cover.

Plants were all of the insect-pollinated type. These pollens which tend to be heavy and sticky are much less likely to become airborne and cause problems.

Obviously, it is wise to garden when the pollen is low. This is likely to be on the cooler, less sunny days and in the morning rather than afternoon. Pollen counts are regularly forecast by the media throughout the spring and summer, so check first before gardening.

If you would like more information in planning a low allergen garden, get in touch with the National Asthma Campaign, who have produced detailed information on the subject. Their booklet *'In the Low Allergy Garden'* tells you the do's and don'ts of gardening and lists the plants, trees, shrubs, vegetables and herbs which are suitable for the person with asthma.

· *Summer storms* ·

Thunderstorms in summer have been known to trigger asthma, sometimes giving rise to attacks that are sufficiently severe to require hospital treatment. Although it is not known what causes these attacks a possibility could be that the summer storms come at a time when the pollen is high. The turbulent weather releases vast quantities of allergens and spores into the atmosphere.

· *Fungi and moulds* ·

The spores from moulds and fungi are another potential hazard. These exist in rooms with rising damp but also can be found in dark, humid and poorly ventilated areas where there is heavy condensation. Keep the house well-ventilated. It helps to clean off any visible mould. Plant mould on houseplants can also present a problem.

· *Food* ·

As a general rule food doesn't seem to be a major factor in asthma with the exception of nuts – peanuts in particular. Nuts have been known to cause serious, even fatal attacks in people with asthma, but these are often due to *anaphylaxis* which is a very severe allergic reaction that causes breathing difficulties and is not true asthma. It is not a common asthma trigger. Artificial colourings, particularly *tartrazine* may produce attacks in some people. *Tartrazine* is an azo dye used commonly in food. It appears in food labelling under its E number – E102. Other azo dyes which could produce problems are sunset yellow (E110), amaranth(123) and ponceau (E124). These can appear in convenience food, smoked food, sweets, chewing gum, squash, fizzy drinks, pickles, sauces, biscuits, cake mixes, jams, soups, jellies, pie fillings, tinned fruit and many others.

Preservatives and flavour enhancers (particularly monosodium glutamate) have also been suggested as possible triggers.

Alcohol is also known to trigger asthma in some people. Red wine is one to watch out for but any alcohol can do it.

However, many asthma experts say that food figures very low in terms of trigger factors. A healthy diet which includes fresh fruit and vegetables, proteins and carbohydrates and dairy products should keep you fit and strong. A diet based on highly processed foods may or may not trigger attacks but it won't do anything for your general health. A well planned diet that builds up your health should make you less prone to picking up infections that can trigger asthma. It should also help you recover from any bad attacks that may come along.

· *Pollution* ·

A number of international studies have claimed that air pollution can cause problems for people with asthma. To date there is no scientific proof that it actually causes the condition in people who do not already have asthma. There was a time when the heavy industrial smogs claimed the lives of thousands of people but the Clean Air Act of 1956 successfully reduced the level of many industrial pollutants like sulphur dioxide (SO_2), which is known to affect people with asthma. Sulphur dioxide is produced when coal is burned. These days power stations are the biggest producers of sulphur dioxide but it can also be created through industrial and domestic use. It causes wheezing particularly if inhaled while exercising.

However, one of the pollutants that is causing the most concern these days is nitrogen dioxide (NO_2) which is produced by car exhaust fumes. 'Nitrogen dioxide paralyses the hairs that line the airways of the lungs and rid them of particulate matter and mucus,' says John Gay, writing in *Asthma News* (Autumn 1993). 'Without them, pollutants stay in the lung for longer periods and the body's sensitivity to infection is greatly increased. This is particularly dangerous for people with asthma, since it adds to the problems of already reduced lung function and scarred lung tissue by clogging the lungs further.' Levels of nitrogen dioxide in the atmosphere increased by 43 per cent in Britain between 1979 and 1989.

Nevertheless, nitrogen dioxide exposure is greatest indoors. In homes with gas fires and gas cookers, it is produced as a by-product of burning natural gas. If you burn natural gas for cooking and heating, properly installed extraction fans and flues combined with good ventilation may reduce the amount of nitrogen dioxide in the air in the home.

Out on the street high levels of nitrogen dioxide can give rise to further pollution. In the presence of ultraviolet, which is part of sunlight, the gas is broken down to form low-level *ozone*. In environmental terms the vital layer which filters out harmful ultraviolet radiation is referred to as the *ozone layer*. Unfortunately, this natural ozone carries out these beneficial functions at very high altitudes, far above the ground level where we breathe the air. Ozone at street level is not good news. It is a highly reactive gas which inflames the airways and reduces the ability of the lungs to work properly and may worsen allergic reactions. This is damaging to anyone's lungs, but in people with asthma it adds to the problems. Escaping to the countryside to avoid this problem may not be the best option. Ozone pollution tends to spread down wind from towns where it is formed, to the countryside where it lurks to afflict unwitting asthma sufferers trying to escape from urban air pollution!

The rise in the use of diesel-powered vehicles has brought an increase in concern about another street-level pollutant known as *particulates* which means tiny pieces of soot, dust or dirt blown by the wind. More diesel-engined trucks are used and the much-heralded ecological benefits of diesel cars has influenced a growing number of motorists to buy them. Unfortunately, it is likely that the increase in the use of these vehicles may be causing an increase in the level of diesel particulates and a rise in asthma symptoms. Although larger particles of 5 microns or more are not carried beyond the mouth and nose, smaller particles down to 0.5 microns, about half the size of an average bacteria can reach the airways.

Normally these would be removed by the natural cleaning processes of the respiratory system but this can be disrupted by the presence of nitrogen dioxide. These particles can remain in the airways and cause irritation to asthmatics. The smallest particles, less than 0.5 microns, can penetrate as far as the *alveoli* in the lungs, where the oxygen in the inhaled air is transferred into the body. These tiny particles can remain there for several years. Such pollution at this level of penetration, combined with pollutant gases, may bring about symptoms in asthma sufferers even when they are removed from the original source of pollution.

These pollutants are, for the time being, an unavoidable by-product of the urban lifestyle which we are increasingly adopting. Environmental awareness may reduce the problem in the future, but for today people with asthma have to learn to live with it. It pays to be aware of the circumstances and situations in which the level of airborne pollutants is likely to be high. If you have asthma and live in an environment where the pollution is constantly high, it is particularly important for you to keep a check on your condition by using the peak-flow meter.

You can find out about pollution levels on a daily basis from *Ceefax* and *Teletext*. The Department of the Environment will also give you information on pollution levels for your area and other areas. They issue warnings if the pollution levels are very high and do, from time to time, suggest that people with asthma stay home on those days or take extra medication. The number for the *Pollution Helpline* you can ring for this information is given in Useful Addresses on page 149.

· *Stress* ·

Centuries ago when we were hunters the body was tuned to quick action stress. When faced with a threatening situation we either stood our ground and fought, or ran. This fight-or-flight response is still part of our physical make-up. When we prepare for action the adrenal glands secrete adrenaline which prepares the body to fight or run. In the old days whether we fought or ran we used up this supply of adrenaline.

Today it is not quite like that. Stress doesn't usually come in the form of a tiger which you fight or run from by scaling up a nearby tree as fast as you can! Stress these days usually has to be contained. You have a bad day at work or somebody on the bus annoys you; although the body is prepared for action there is no physical outlet for the adrenaline. This can happen day in and day out for months and years. Sometimes the stress 'comes out' as it were, in illnesses like asthma, eczema, migraine, ulcerative colitis and so on. So it is worth looking at ways of coping with stress in our current lives. However, it should be said that stress is not considered to be a cause of asthma but it can aggravate the condition.

Obviously if you can identify the cause of the stress and get rid of some or all of it, that's going to be a very real help, but even so, it is highly unlikely that you are going to lead an entirely stress-free life.

There are many ways of coping with stress and tension. Meditation, relaxation techniques and yoga are some. Certainly, if you have asthma it is well worth finding a way of calming down and relaxing that you can call upon when you are becoming tense. But I think it is very important to bear in mind that one good way of getting rid of stress is by doing something you like, and you don't need to have asthma to benefit from that.

Promote enjoyment and demote the 'musts' and 'oughts' in life as much as you can. If you are an adult with asthma this means finding time to do the things you like. If you enjoy any type of sport, listening to music, going to the theatre, reading a book or whatever – do it regularly, as often as you can and if that means saying goodbye to a 'must' or an 'ought to', so be it.

If you are the parent of a child with asthma, promote this principle in your household. In as much as the whole family is affected by a child with asthma, they should all be considered when the treats are being handed around. Pay special attention to the things that each child in the family, whether they have asthma or not, enjoys doing and try your hardest to make sure each gets to do it as often as they possibly can. And apply the same principle to yourself and your spouse.

If you feel constantly guilty and believe you cannot have treats unless you've earned them, accept that if you've got asthma, or are caring for someone who has, you've earned all the goodies you can get! But better than that, bear in mind that enjoying yourself is a good antidote to stress and if you don't do the first from time to time you could wind-up with an overload of the second.

One of the most stressful things in your life could be the fear of an asthma attack. The way around this is to know as much as you can about the condition, particularly as it affects you. Get into a management plan that you can handle relatively easily. Have clear in your mind exactly what you can and would do in an emergency. The more in control you are of your asthma the more confident you will be that you can handle any crisis that may arise. This is bound to minimise the fear and the stress attached to it.

· *Exercise* ·

Exercise that triggers asthma is known as exercise-induced asthma. Although everyone gets breathless after rigorous exercise, the person with asthma will start wheezing and coughing and feel that their chest is tightening. This can happen a minute after stopping the exercise and last for up to half an hour. If this occurs it is important to see your doctor and get it diagnosed. It does not mean that you have to give up sport and exercise – quite the contrary, it is good to stay fit and sport is a good way of achieving that. What you will need to do is to take precautions against an exercise-induced attack.

It is generally thought that the temperature and moisture content of the air, combined with exercise, is what triggers these attacks. Cold, dry air is certainly a trigger for some people. Warm, moist air does not seem to constitute such a problem. You will also be more prone to an exercise-induced attack after an infection, like a cold, when your airways are particularly sore. Pollen, is of course, another trigger and if you are exercising outside when the pollen count is high, you will be more susceptible to an attack than on other occasions.

Long periods of exercise seem to produce more problems than short bursts. So running in a marathon on a cold, dry day could surely spell trouble for an asthma patient. A game of tennis on a hard court on a warm day may not pose a problem.

Swimming is a sport which is very popular with asthma sufferers. Swimming in an indoor pool where the air is warm and moist is not likely to trigger an attack unless, of course, the person is sensitive to chlorine. It is the atmospheric conditions that render it okay – the humidity of the air surrounding the pool. If you were to take a dip in the sea on Christmas Day this would not be a safe swim!

There are ways to protect yourself from symptoms of exercise-induced asthma. According to the National Asthma Campaign, taking several 30 second sprints over a period of 5-10 minutes before beginning a vigorous sport can sometimes protect the lungs for an hour or so.

Although as a rule you do not use your reliever medicine to prevent an attack, before exercise the reliever can act as a preventer. Two puffs of the reliever medicine is what is often prescribed and is usually very effective. *Intal* can also be taken, if prescribed, before exercising and it can work in these circumstances. However, it will not help you once the wheezing has started. You will need to use a reliever drug instead.

Please don't give up exercising or doing a sport you enjoy because of asthma. And if you have a child with asthma encourage him or her to take part in as many sporting activities as is reasonably safe.

NB: *All asthma patients should always carry their reliever inhalers with them during sport or exercise.*

Obviously it makes sense to avoid long periods of strenuous exercise on cold, dry days. But exercise not only keeps you fit, it also helps reduce stress which is another trigger factor.

Some of our best and most famous sports people have asthma. If they can do it, so can you!

· *Infection* ·

Viral infections like colds and flu can often cause severe asthma attacks because they damage the airways and increase the inflammation. If you have a virus it is particularly important to take peak-flow readings so that you can see, at the earliest opportunity, whether or not your asthma is deteriorating. Your doctor may prescribe an anti-inflammatory drug to clear things up quickly.

Sinus infections can also have a detrimental effect on asthma and need to be treated. Bacterial infections are unlikely to provoke asthma attacks. Antibiotics which are used to treat these kinds of infection are very rarely effective in treating asthma.

· *Medicines* ·

There are drugs that are known to trigger asthma in susceptible people. These are aspirin, some medicines prescribed for heart diseases, some drugs for arthritis, non-steroid anti-inflammatory drugs like *Bupfrofen* and some eye drops used for treating glaucoma. People with asthma should be wary of taking beta-blockers as they can trigger serious and sometimes fatal attacks. Always remind your doctor that you are an asthma patient.

· *Chemicals* ·

Household and DIY products that are solvent-based can cause problems with people with asthma. These include glues, varnishes, paints, paint-cleaning fluids and dry-cleaning products. The solvents evaporate into the air giving rise to vapours which can inflame sensitised lungs. Water-based varnishes and paints are a safer bet because although they do contain chemicals that can irritate (like ammonia) they are there in much smaller concentrations. Formaldehyde which can be present in urea/phenol-formaldehyde resin glues used in the manufacture of some wood-based panel products, such as chipboard, and some foam-backed carpets can cause problems: so can some wood preservatives. If you want to know more about these and other pollutants you can acquire a free booklet *Good Air Quality in your Home* from The Department of the Environment (see Useful Addresses on page 149).

6

Doctors, Clinics and Hospitals

The majority of people who have asthma are treated in the doctor's surgery. Moreover, it is estimated that 87 per cent of attacks are treated by the GP. So doctor's surgeries are of prime importance in asthma management.

When you see a doctor for the first time with symptoms of asthma he or she will aim to make a diagnosis. As has been explained in Chapter 1 there are different ways of doing this. The doctor will first want to know the symptoms you are experiencing and if there are any particular times when they are worse. He may ask if symptoms arise particularly when you are in the garden, in a smoky atmosphere, after exercise, or when the air is very cold, windy and so on. The doctor will then be interested in your family history. Does anyone else suffer from asthma? Do you or any of your near relatives suffer from eczema, hay fever or allergic rhinitis?

By taking this kind of medical history the doctor can see whether you are genetically predisposed to asthma and whether the common triggers set it off. This will give him a pretty good idea as to whether or not the condition you have is asthma.

The peak-flow meter is another diagnostic tool. It is a measure of how well you can breathe out and this is related to how narrow your tubes are. Although it is a very useful way of diagnosing asthma it has its drawbacks as a one-off diagnosis in the surgery. First of all, you may have been having a few minor symptoms which prompted you to make a doctor's appointment. But by the time you see the doctor the symptoms have subsided and your is breathing normal. So the peak-flow reading will register a normal reading, but you may, in fact, have asthma. You don't have to experience symptoms continuously to have the condition.

To get over this the doctor may induce narrowing of the airways by putting you through an exercise test. If the test is positive and brings on the symptoms it is an indication of asthma, particularly if there is a history of atopic conditions in the family and there are other asthma triggers that induce the symptoms.

But not everybody who has asthma responds to the exercise test. So if the doctor suspects that your symptoms are asthma what he will probably do is to send you home with a chart and a peak-flow meter. You will be asked to record your peak-flow readings morning and evening and enter them on a chart. (This is explained in Chapter 3). You will probably be asked to do this over a period of two weeks. What the doctor is looking for is a variability of more than 15 per cent in your readings. If at the end of two weeks the doctor studies your chart and sees that your peak-flow varies from one time in the day to another time in the day by more than 15 per cent, he will, in all probability, diagnose asthma.

Sometimes doctors use anti-asthma drugs to confirm the condition. Drugs prescribed for asthma are designed to improve your peak-flow and, of course, clear the symptoms. If the doctor suspects you have asthma, he may try you on anti-asthma medicine. If your symptoms clear as a result of this treatment, asthma is likely to be diagnosed. But it may mean taking the drugs for a good few weeks before results are achieved and the diagnosis confirmed.

· *Treatment* ·

If you are given a peak-flow meter make sure you know how to use it and find out when you should come back for another consultation. If you are given asthma medicine ask the doctor what the treatment is that is being offered, when you should use it, how often and what you can expect it to do. Don't try and remember all the doctor says. Write it down or ask the doctor to write it down.

Asthma treatment is, on the whole, very straightforward. In 1992 a number of interested parties got together to produce a set of guidelines in asthma management. Their aim is to get health professionals throughout the world to manage asthma in very much the same way. The guidelines also give doctors and hospital staff a very clear picture of how to treat asthma patients depending on whether the person is a child or an adult and taking into consideration the severity of the condition. So there should be very little guess work involved in treating asthma these days.

The guidelines, which have been issued by the British Thoracic Society (BTS) who are chest specialists, have been devised by a group of professional bodies which include: The British Paediatric Association, the Research Unit of the Royal College of Physicians of London, the King's Fund Centre, the National Asthma Campaign, the Royal College of General Practitioners, the General Practitioners in Asthma Group, the British Association of Accident and Emergency Medicine, the British Paediatric Respiratory Group as well as, of course, the British Thoracic Society themselves.

The guidelines give a clear indication of the different steps in treating asthma according to the level of severity of the illness. Here is a summary of these steps.

- **Step one:** At this level only reliever treatment is used and this is on an occasional basis. If the reliever is needed more than once a day, step two is indicated providing the patient knows how to use the inhaler properly and *is* using it
- **Step two:** At this step the patient will be offered an inhaled steroid to be used twice a day or, less likely, an anti-inflammatory medicine such as *cromoglycate* or *nedocromil*. This is in addition to the quick-acting reliever which is used as required.
- **Step three:** Here a much higher dose of inhaled steroid is prescribed, usually used through a spacer. There are a few patients who experience problems with a high dose of inhaled steroids and they would be offered alternative treatment. Quick-acting bronchodilators (relievers) are used as required.

The aim of these three steps of treatment is to manage asthma to the extent that there are little or no chronic symptoms, including those that occur at night. There is minimum use of reliever inhalers and there are no limitations on what people can do, including exercise. There are very infrequent attacks, and it is hoped, no acute ones.

- **Step four:** In addition to the high dose of inhaled steroids, quick-acting bronchodilators are used on a regular basis. The patient may also be prescribed another drug to help manage the condition and this could be one of several including *ipratropium, cromoglycate, nedocromil,* the long-acting relievers, *theophylline,* or high dose bronchodilator.
- **Step five:** At this stage steroid tablets (*prednisolone*) will be prescribed to be taken regularly. In addition the patient will be taking inhaled steroids through a spacer, one or more of the long-acting bronchodilators as well as the inhaled quick-acting reliever as required.

In these last two steps the ideal outcome is to keep symptoms to a minimum, keep the use of relievers down and limit activity as little as possible. The aim is to do all this as well as achieve the least possible adverse effects from the medicine.

- **Stepping down:** The aim of asthma management is to match the treatment to the severity of the condition. So just as there may be a need to step up treatment if the condition deteriorates, so there is equal concern to reduce it down when the situation has improved and can be stabilised at the lower level. The guidelines advise reviewing treatment every three to six months or earlier, particularly at Steps four and five.

A very small minority of patients cannot be controlled through using these guidelines.

· *Asthma clinics* ·

Ten or fifteen years ago very few doctors' surgeries included nurses. These days most surgeries have practice nurses who are taking on new roles. They run family planning clinics, advise on travel medicine and also run asthma clinics. Assuming that the practice nurses running asthma clinics have received appropriate training there is not a great deal of difference between seeing them and a GP.

It is not always the case, but you may find that the practice nurse may have more time to offer. A doctor in a busy surgery will have a limited amount of time to see each patient. A nurse who is running a specialised clinic may have more time for each patient. Also the latter will know that she (or he) is going to be talking about asthma for that dedicated period of time. This means that she can focus on the subject completely and access the information she needs. A doctor who may have seen half-a-dozen patients with diverse ailments in the past hour may not be focused on asthma in quite the same way. It is likely that both will be following the guidelines for treatment already described.

Whether you are seeing a doctor or asthma nurse it is usually better if you can see the same person each time. This way he or she will get to know quite a bit about you, your asthma and your previous treatment. They will know what has worked and what hasn't. Have you had to step up treatment or have you been able to reduce it? Establishing an ongoing therapeutic relationship with a health professional can be beneficial in helping you manage your asthma.

· *Changing doctors* ·

If you are not happy with your doctor or the level of care you are offered at your GP practice, it is worth knowing that it is really very easy to change. All you have to do is to find another doctor to take you on. Do a bit of research. See what other practices have to offer. If there is a surgery that you know is good or have heard good things about, make an appointment with one of the senior doctors. Tell him or her that asthma is a particular concern of yours and find out the kind of care that is offered to asthma patients – children and adult – in that practice. How do the doctors feel about being called out in the early hours of the morning? Make a list of the things that concern you about your asthma treatment and go through them with the doctor.

Don't worry about asking these kinds of questions. People are often very worried about asking too many questions and wasting the doctor's time. Bear in mind that a doctor who is patient with your questioning is also likely to be patient and understanding of the vagaries of your asthma.

Assuming you have found a doctor to whom you want to change, first make sure that the practice is willing to take you on. If they are, you must now write to your current doctor and tell him that you are moving and where you are moving to. This is so that your medical records are sent on to the new practice. You don't have to give the out-going doctor any reasons for your move. You will then need to wait a couple of weeks for your medical records to reach their new destination – and that's it.

If you would like any more information on changing doctors you can ring the Regional Health Information Service (see Useful Addresses on page 149). This service can also give you waiting times for different operations in hospitals in your region as well as self-help groups in your area. If you want to know how to make a comment or complaint about the health service, operators on this line can usually point you in the right direction to get help.

· *Hospitals* ·

A lot of people are first diagnosed with asthma when they wind up in casualty. This happens particularly with small children when the parent hasn't realised that the coughing could be asthma. If you, or your child, are first diagnosed with asthma in the casualty department of a hospital, you need to see your doctor the next day to tell him what has happened. You may need further treatment and in any event the fact that you or your child has asthma needs to be noted in the medical records.

Treatment in the Accident and Emergency department of a hospital is covered in the British Thoracic Society guidelines already mentioned. Staff have a detailed guide as to treatment to give, depending on the severity of the symptoms, when it is all right to discharge you or when they need to admit you into hospital.

· *Skin prick tests* ·

In this test a solution is made up that contains a small amount of a possible allergy-creating substance such as cat dander, house dust mite or pollen. This is introduced into the skin by gently pricking it with a sterile needle and dropping the solution into the slightly opened area. The idea is that if you are allergic to the substance the body will react by producing a weal. Skin tests do not work very well with asthma. What produces an allergy in the skin may not affect the lungs or the nasal passages. So skin tests are not considered very effective in finding out what triggers symptoms in a particular patient.

· *In-patient treatment* ·

If you are admitted into hospital the staff will not only be concerned with opening up your airways, but they will also be treating the inflammation.

What has happened in the attack is that your tubes have become inflamed and narrowed. To bring the inflammation down you will be put on a course of steroid tablets. However, it takes about 8 hours before the steroids start to work so in the meantime the constriction in your airways has to be treated. This is done, of course, with big doses of bronchodilator to open them up.

One of the problems with people treating themselves at home with nebulisers is that they open up the airways, but unless they seek medical advice at the same time, they are not treating the condition. So as soon as the nebuliser treatment is stopped the asthma deteriorates again.

In hospital the doctors and nurses will be giving you both preventer and reliever treatment. Again the BTS guidelines indicate what to give. Often people are kept on regular nebulisers, sometimes every four hours, so that while the steroids are taking time to work the airways are kept open. But what they want to see before they send you home from hospital is that when they've stopped the nebuliser and put you on the treatment that you will be having at home, you stay well on it. They not only want to see that the peak-flow has improved now but that it will stay that way even when the high doses of bronchodilator have stopped. So while you're in hospital the reliever medicine is likely to be reduced so that you can be observed while you're on your normal level of medication.

Increasingly in hospitals there are 'liaison nurses'. These are nurses who may see you in hospital when you're admitted but will also visit you at home when you are discharged to see how well the treatment is working.

· *Hospital clinics* ·

These work along very similar lines to the clinics run by nurses in doctor's surgeries. Sometimes the patients are people who have come in as an emergency and are now attending the clinic so that they can learn to manage their condition better and prevent another similar attack. But generally speaking patients attending hospital asthma clinics are usually people whose condition is difficult to control and they need the specialist expertise that the hospital staff can offer.

The nurses in attendance at these clinics are likely to be respiratory nurses and chest nurses who have a great deal of experience in asthma.

7

ASTHMA AT WORK

For several years in the 1980s Barcelona was struck by what seemed to be an epidemic of asthma. It came in regular bouts. Every so often the emergency departments of the city's hospitals would be flooded with patients experiencing acute asthma attacks. Why this was happening no one knew but extensive research was dedicated to finding out. Eventually it was discovered that most of the cases of asthma during these bouts came from in and around the harbour area. Furthermore, the timings of the epidemics coincided with the days on which cargoes of soya beans were being unloaded in the harbour. The fine dust from the beans was being blown around the area and also further inland. Susceptible people who were unwittingly inhaling this dust were experiencing symptoms of asthma. Putting lids on the soya-bean silos helped ease the problem.

People who already have asthma may become tight-chested or wheezy if they are exposed to triggers at work. The already sensitive airways are likely to react to the irritant or allergen and produce asthma symptoms.

However it is also possible that airborne substances inhaled while working can actually cause asthma in someone who previously did not have the condition. These substances are known, in these cases, as *respiratory sensitisers* and this type of asthma is referred to as 'occupational'. If you have been exposed to sensitisers during the course of your job your lungs may have become sensitised as a result. This means that you have become prone to asthma symptoms, and the problem is that once the disposition to asthma has been switched on, it can be difficult, or impossible, to switch it off again.

· *Occupational asthma* ·

Research funded by the National Asthma Campaign has shown that the more a person is exposed to a respiratory sensitiser, the greater the risk is that he or she will develop symptoms of asthma. Also, if the sensitiser which is causing the problems is identified early on and the worker is then either protected or removed from it, it is believed there is a good chance that the asthma will disappear.

However, a worker who has been exposed to an inhaled sensitiser over a long period of time is likely to experience increasingly severe asthma symptoms and the chances of their disappearing are not very high. Even if the worker changes jobs and is no longer exposed to the sensitiser he or she is likely to continue to require asthma treatment. Furthermore, once the lungs have been sensitised and the asthma has been switched on, the person becomes susceptible to other triggers which can induce asthma.

It also needs to be said that occupational asthma can take several months or even years to develop.

In 1982 The Department of Health and Social Security (DHSS) recognised occupational asthma as a 'prescribed disease'. If you suffer from such a disease you can get compensation for the ill health you are experiencing. There is a list of respiratory sensitisers for which you can claim compensation from the Department of Social Security (DSS) and these are listed at the end of this chapter. The list gets updated from time to time so it is worth checking with the DSS if you are in any doubt.

How do you know if your asthma has been caused by a substance you are exposed to at work? Here are two questions you might like to consider:

- Is your asthma is worse during the week, not necessarily while you are at work, but during the course of the working week? It will often get worse after leaving work and sometimes you may find that the symptoms interrupt your sleep.
- Does your asthma improve when you are not at work, particularly when you have been away from work for several days, for example on holiday?

It is very important in suspected cases of occupational asthma that careful evidence is collected so the doctor involved has the necessary knowledge to help. If your GP is not sure what to do it may be an idea to ask for referral to a specialist.

Claiming Compensation

You may be eligible for compensation for occupational asthma if one of the respiratory sensitisers is found at work and if it is thought likely that sensitisation to this substance has caused your asthma.

If you believe that you may be suffering from occupational asthma you can start investigating further in one of two ways. You can see your doctor who may arrange for you to have tests at a hospital. Or you can get an information leaflet from your local DSS called *Occupational Asthma* (leaflet NI 237) which will give you more information.

If you feel that you could be eligible for compensation get form BI 100 (OA) from your local DSS office, fill it in and return it. Also, the National

Asthma Campaign's leaflet *Asthma at Work* discusses occupational asthma and eligibility for compensation.

If the DSS decides that you may be eligible for compensation you may be invited to go to a Medical Boarding Centre (Respiratory Diseases). There you will be examined by two doctors who will also refer to your GP or hospital for more evidence. If they decide that you have occupational asthma which has been caused by one of the respiratory sensitisers on their list, they will then have to make a decision as to how disabled you are. You should hear within a few weeks.

If you do not agree with either the diagnosis or assessment of your disability, you can take the matter up with a Medical Appeal Tribunal. This tribunal is independent of the DSS and has a legal chairman as well as two hospital chest consultants.

What compensation you receive is dependent on the level of your disability. If it is assessed at 14 per cent or more you will be entitled to a 'disablement benefit' which is paid as a weekly pension. This disablement pension is usually reviewed every year or two by the Medical Boarding Centre on the grounds that the condition can improve or deteriorate.

If you find that your asthma has worsened before the provisional award finishes, you can apply to the DSS again on the grounds of 'unforeseen aggravation'.

There are other benefits you may be entitled to besides a disablement benefit. Disability Living Allowance and Disability Working Allowance are two that are briefly described in the A-Z of Asthma at the end of this book. Neither requires you to have occupational asthma. The DSS pamphlet *Occupational Asthma* already mentioned also gives details.

Preventing occupational asthma

It is possible sometimes to replace substances which are known to cause asthma with safer ones. This is obviously the best action, but if it cannot be achieved the next best step is to protect the workers. This can be done by sealing off any equipment which produces hazardous substances so that these sensitisers are not inhaled by the workforce. Ensuring that workers wear masks and protective clothing can reduce the exposure level. Fitting extractor fans can also be helpful. If you've moved to a different part of the building it is worth knowing that you may still be vulnerable as respiratory sensitisers may have been carried in the air or on other workers' clothes to the new area.

General working conditions

Working conditions as a whole can have a marked bearing on the symptoms of someone with asthma. Good ventilation is important in dispersing pollutants and can also help keep down the spread of viral infections. However, the biggest problem in this area is cigarette smoke. (See Michelle's story later in this chapter.) *Passive smoking* is a known hazard to anyone and tobacco smoke is a known irritant to people with asthma. More and more employers are making their workplace no-smoking areas, but those that don't should ensure that smoking is restricted to limited areas only, so that their entire workforce is not exposed to this hazardous pollutant.

High-risk jobs

The most hazardous jobs in terms of asthma are considered to be those of spray painters, chemical processors, plastics workers, bakers, metal treaters, laboratory workers, welders, solderers and assemblers. You will see the reasons why when you look at the list of hazardous substances given below.

In addition you may find a career in the armed services, police, fire brigade and ambulance services inadvisable or even, perhaps, closed to you if you have asthma because of the potentially harmful circumstances in which you may find yourself during the course of your work.

· Respiratory sensitisers ·

You may be able to claim compensation if you have been exposed to the following substances during the course of your work:

- *Isocyanates* used in polyurethane foam manufacture and spray painting.
- *Platinum salts* encountered in platinum refining.
- *Epoxy Resin* curing agents and hardening agents. These include *phthalic anhydride, tetrachlorophtalic anhydride, trimellitic anhydride* or *triethylenetretramine* which are all used in paint manufacture.
- *Colophony fumes arising from the use of rosin as a soldering flux* used in the electronics industry,
- *Proteolytic enzymes* used in the detergent industry.
- *Dust arising from the sowing, cultivation, harvesting, drying, handling, milling, transport or storage of barley, oats, rye, wheat, maize or the handling, transport or storage of flour made from them.* Bakers, millers and farmers, among others, will be exposed to these substances.
- *Antibiotics and cimetidine* implicated in drug manufacture.

- *Wood dust, for example cedar and mahogany.* Carpenters, joiners, papermill and sawmill workers would be exposed to this.
- *Isphagula dust.* This is a component of bulk laxatives and workers employed in the manufacture as well as administrators (nurses for example) may be exposed to it.
- *Castor bean dust* may come into the orbit of merchant seamen, laboratory workers and felt makers.
- *Ipecacuanha* is used in the preparation of ipecacuanha tablets.
- *Azodicarbonamide* is a blowing agent in the manufacture of expanded foam plastics.
- *Glutaraldehyde* in hospitals (used as disinfectant, and in connection with histology and electron microscopy). Also in leather tanning and cooling towers.
- *Persulphate salts and henna* used in hairdressing.
- *Animals including insects, other arthropods and their larvae* may affect laboratory workers who work with them and pest controllers as well as people involved in fruit cultivation.
- *Crustaceans or fish or their products,* involved in food processing.
- *Reactive dyes* involved in textile manufacture.
- *Soya bean* involved in food processing.
- *Tea dust and green coffee dust* involved in foodprocessing.
- *Fumes from stainless steel welding.*
- *Any other sensitising agent inhaled at work.* This category may be used where there is good expert medical evidence for an unusual or new sensitising agent.

· *A case history* ·

Peter ran a very successful bakery for all his working life. He came from a family of master bakers. His grandfather and father had both worked in the business and when he came home from the War, Peter was expected to join the family firm.

During the course of his working life Peter developed allergic rhinitis. This was thought to be due to the flour dust to which he was constantly exposed. It got to the stage where he had to wear a mask all the time he was at work and he treated the symptoms with a nasal spray. Apart from that his health was fine.

It was not until some time after he had retired, in his late-sixties, that Peter's asthma symptoms came on. Very quickly his asthma became so severe that he was on a maintenance dose of oral steroids as well as steroid inhalers and high doses of bronchodilators.

The degree of his asthma was such that it greatly interfered with his life. He was afraid of getting acute attacks when he was away from home.

Although more controlled now, Peter's asthma is still severe. This is inspite of the fact that he has been retired for over 10 years and away from the flour dust which probably induced the condition.

· *Personal accounts* ·

The following two personal accounts are not strictly of occupational asthma but focus on working and asthma.

· MICHELLE ·

I've had asthma for about three and a half years. I'm 27 years old now. The asthma came on over a period of about four or five months. I work as a delivery driver and as I was driving around in the firm's van. I found I was getting drowsy, not feeling very well and I was having difficulty in breathing. I was also getting very wheezy and I found it hard to sleep at night. I didn't know what was causing it until a colleague of mine drove the same van and he felt the drowsiness. We examined the van and checked the seals and found that there was an inch gap on the back doors. The diesel fumes were coming in.

I think that's what set off my asthma. I never had a hint of it before that time although my mother does suffer from asthma. I went to the doctor who first thought it might be a chest infection. He gave me some antibiotics which helped a bit but didn't clear it up. He then did a peak-flow reading in the surgery and gave me some Ventolin after that. I found it easier to breathe immediately after I'd taken the Ventolin. He diagnosed asthma.

The doctor felt it could have been the pollution I had been breathing in that triggered it off. But since there was no proof there was nothing much I could do about it.

The firm fixed the van, but unfortunately now that it's been triggered I can't get shot of the asthma. I am now on Becotide, two puffs twice a day, as well as the Ventolin as and when I need it.

I've only really had one asthma attack as such. I did the thing you shouldn't do – I panicked. My alarm went off for work in the morning. I could feel that my chest was really tight – worse than normal. I took my Becotide. That doesn't clear it right away; it's just a preventative. Then I took two puffs of the Ventolin and there was no effect at all. There was no easing of anything. I could feel my chest getting tighter and tighter and I was beginning to panic a bit because it wasn't working and I couldn't understand why. It always had in the past and I was really struggling to get my breath.

After a few minutes I started trying to calm myself down and I found that the more I relaxed the easier it got. And once I got myself calmed down I used the Ventolin again and it eventually started to ease. I managed to sort it out on my own. I didn't have to call the doctor or anything. I managed to get to work that morning. I was just a bit late.

I know I haven't got asthma badly. I've never been hospitalised. But it has affected my working life in some ways. I have to do a lot of lifting and jumping in and out of the van and running up and down stairs. I find that I get out of breath a lot more quickly than I used to before asthma came into my life. I don't dare go out without my inhaler. I take one everywhere I go. I have a spare one at work and I keep one in the van all the time. I have a spare one in the house as well.

At the moment I don't do long-distance driving. The most I do is a four-hour round trip. As long as I've got my inhaler it doesn't worry me. I have a mobile phone as well. I know if I run into any difficulties I can get in touch with somebody.

I find I'm worse in damp weather because I'm more prone to chest infections then. If I have a cold it goes right on to my chest and that brings on the asthma. I walk to and from work and it's over a mile each way. I take my inhaler before I go and by the time I get to work I have to take my inhaler again. If it's really windy I find it very hard to catch my breath. It's better when it's cold and crisp. I do catch my breath a little bit then but not half as much as when it is raining or windy.

The air pollution here in Cumbria doesn't seem half as bad as elsewhere. I find that the air quality has a lot to do with my asthma. I know that when I'm in London it really is bad. I have to use my inhaler all the time. I think if I was living in London I would be a lot worse.

If I go into a very smoky pub or if I drink red wine I'm in trouble. With a certain amount of alcohol I can feel my chest tighten, but red wine is the worst and I love red wine. I can have a couple of glasses and then I have to stay off it.

I find that smoke really affects me and there are staff in the office who smoke. Luckily I am out most of the time but if I do spend a full day in the office I have difficulty in breathing at the end of it. It's not like that when I'm out and about in the van. I have asked very nicely if they could restrict their smoking to either a smaller office which is not used much or have a smoking room. Both of these things could be achieved quite easily but they don't want to know. They say it would be too inconvenient. So I'm in a no-win situation where smoking is concerned.

We don't allow anyone to smoke in the house and, of course, we don't smoke either. Any visitors who do have to smoke outside.

I try not to let asthma affect the way I lead my life because I think you can cripple yourself more by the thought of not being able to do things. I have to try and stay away from dust. If I'm cleaning and I overdo it I find I have to stop to get my breath and take my inhaler. My husband does most of that kind of housework.

Asthma doesn't stop me from doing anything that I want to do. Obviously I have to make sure that I take the Becotide daily and I have my inhaler with me all the time. But I have a positive way of thinking about it. I've got asthma but I've got to get on with it. Just because you've got asthma it doesn't mean you can't live your life exactly as you want. But I do know that it's different for people who have asthma really badly. I know it can stop them from doing things.

· BRIAN ·

Brian had his first asthma attack ten years ago when he was 40 years old. He is a workaholic who runs his own transport company. At one time he headed a large business which ran 75 wagons and 200 trailers. His company has since reduced in size – not due to his asthma but because of pressure from the bank. As you will gather from his story, Brian has not let asthma get in the way of his leading a very full life. He has a pilot's licence and owns a seven-seater, twin engine aeroplane. Sunday lunch is not necessarily a trip to the local but, occasionally, a flight over the channel to Le Touquet! Here is his story.

I started with asthma in 1984. I was off work for eight weeks with it. I was given a lot of steroids. They got it under control. I've been on Ventolin and Becloforte ever since. It came on suddenly. I'd never had it as a child.

I think what brought it on was stress. I was running about 30 wagons then. Overnight, because of many pressures I thought I was going to lose the business. I was frightened of going bust. I tend to worry about things. I tend to worry about the way my wagons look. The way they are. That's why I'm here seven days a week.

My business survived in 1984 and by 1990 I was running 75 wagons and 200 trailers that employed between 80 and 90 people. It was a mega business. My asthma was not a problem. I had it under control. But a new bank manager came and reduced my overdraft to a point where you couldn't run a large company on that kind of money. And then there was the Gulf War which doubled the price of fuel.

When they pulled the plug on my business my asthma got out of control. It was the stress and the worry of it all. I'd started this business in 1966 with an old 1949 lorry and £75 in a Trustee Savings Bank. I'd just worked and worked and worked. They put me on a nebuliser. I went through another course of Prednisolone [oral steroids]. I started off on about 30mg a day followed by a reducing dose.

Now when I feel an attack coming on I take my Ventolin, get that down me, wait for about 10 minutes and then give myself some Becloforte. And then I'm right.

I went to see a herbalist and if I had taken any notice of him I'd have starved to death. 'Don't eat cheese,' he said. 'You can't have fat.' Everything I liked I couldn't have. So I thanked him, paid him the money and then forgot all about it.

Being out on the roads has made it difficult. One day I was making a delivery to a chocolate factory in York. I had left my Ventolin at home. I could feel an attack coming on. The worry of not having my Ventolin inhaler made it come on worse. One of the workers at the factory took me to the medical. The nurse had gone to do some shopping. They sat me outside on a chair and bleeped the nurse. She came back and gave me two or three puffs of Ventolin that they had there and it cleared it. Now I've got Ventolin inhalers hidden everywhere. I hide one in the wagon, one in the car and in the office. As soon as the stocks start getting low I ring the doctors. I want the security of having the inhalers. I'm also stocked up with steroids. If I think I need a course I'll have a course.

What I have noticed is that every time I get a cold or flu it brings the phlegm on which makes it worse. Since I've had the flu jab I've felt a lot better. I'm not getting colds and flu now which always used to put me down in the dumps. I had no energy for the job. I've been a lot more enthusiastic in the job. I'm a lot better in myself. And I'm very confident about being able to control my asthma.

When my business went down I started up again. I was not going to lie down for anybody. But I'm only running six wagons now. I preferred running a big company.

I love flying. I used to have a two-seater but I sold it and bought a seven-seater. I fly to France. I'll go on a jolly somewhere. The Civil Aviation Authority know I've got asthma. As long as I've got it under control they'll let me fly. They suspended my licence in 1984 when I was bad. But when my doctor wrote to the CAA doctors and said it was under control they gave my licence back to me again. I've never been worried about flying. I love it. When I retire I would like to go on a flying holiday.

8

ASPECTS OF LIVING

As with any chronic condition, asthma can effect you in different ways in different situations and at various stages of your life. Going on holiday, for instance, may need to be planned with asthma in mind, particularly if the condition is severe. If you travel equipped with the medicines you need in the event of an attack and feel that you can cope with one, should it happen, you are much more likely to relax and enjoy your holiday than if you go unprepared and worried.

Similarly with sport and exercise. Keeping fit is an important aspect of anyone's life. If you have asthma it is certainly beneficial to keep as healthy as possible, not only to guard against infections that may provoke an attack, but to build up your strength to recuperate quicker should you experience one. But what if exercise provokes your asthma – should you give it a miss or are there ways to prevent an exercise-induced attack? There certainly are and this chapter details those.

Asthma experienced in pregnancy will bring with it certain anxieties and fears and these may be very different to the kinds of problems that accompany asthma experienced, perhaps for the first time, in old age. In this chapter we look at some of the aspects of living with asthma in different situations. You may also like to look at the A-Z of asthma at the end of this book for ideas on coping with asthma in different situations.

· *Holidays* ·

The success of any holiday usually depends on how carefully it is planned, and this is even more the case when you have to take a condition like asthma into consideration. Perhaps the most important thing to bear in mind before you go on holiday is that you must be sure to **take all your usual medicaments with you plus some extra** in case of eventualities.

If your asthma has been a bit active recently it is well worth making an appointment with your doctor to discuss a holiday plan. He or she may suggest that you increase the dose of your preventers for the period immediately before your holiday to give you a little extra protection. You may also be advised to take some steroid tablets with you in case your asthma gets worse while you are away. This should help settle things down until you come home. Certainly, keeping a peak-flow chart is a good idea on holiday. This way you can be alerted to a deterioration in your condition straightaway, take preventative treatment and in so doing perhaps avoid emergency treatment in unfamiliar surroundings.

It can be worth taking location into consideration if you are particularly susceptible to certain triggers. If, for example, cold air and exercise is a problem for you, a skiing holiday may not be a good choice. On the other hand, many people with asthma do go skiing and enjoy it. Certainly if the house dust mite is your particular trigger and you don't have a problem with cold air, a ski resort would be good for you because the house dust mite does not survive in those climatic conditions.

Similarly, if you cannot tolerate heat and dust stay away from hot dusty locations. Pollution is another factor you might like to consider. There are some parts of the Far East where the pollution is high, and you may need to give those places a miss. High humidity can pose a problem for some people, so again that is worth thinking about. Some people find breeze sets off their asthma so a location set on a windy sea front would not be an ideal choice under these circumstances.

If you are planning to fly you can check with the airline to see if they carry nebulisers. It is worth finding this out before you book.

Booking your holiday through a well established and well-informed travel agent could give you peace of mind. Go through all the points of concern carefully before booking and don't get hurried or pressurised into making a quick decision. Holidays are expensive and your health is precious, so on those two counts alone you should give yourself time to make up your mind.

Check that your insurance policy covers asthma as some do not. If yours doesn't shop around until you find one that does.

Camping and caravanning can be fun and this type of holiday is usually low on the dust mite factor. But it can put you more into contact with pollens and dust and sometimes animals.

Cruises are a good option if you can afford them. Pets and pollens don't pose a problem but check before you book that the cruise liner is medically well equipped.

Here are some more holiday pointers you might like to consider:

● Spinhalers and Rotahalers do not work as well in hot, humid climates so you may need to take the equivalent in a different type of container.
● Before you go check that you have all your usual inhalers, preventers and relievers and make sure you have more than enough to see you through. Take your peak-flow meter and you may need to take standby medicine like oral steroids. If you use a nebuliser you should take that along with any adaptor you may need in order to use it in a foreign country. Your travel agent can advise you on this. If you have a battery operated nebuliser, don't forget to take spare batteries!

- It is a good idea to take a list of your medications with you. If you are travelling in Europe don't forget to take your *E111* form.
- Ask your doctor to give you a letter saying that you have asthma and that the drugs you are carrying with you are for your personal use and you need to have them ready to hand in case of emergency. This may obviate any problems you may have in keeping your inhalers in the cabin with you on the airline. It should also guard against the unlikely event of your medication being confiscated by customs officials. However, while the doctor's letter may help, it won't be a guarantee, so check on the rules of the airline and what the customs situation is likely to be in the country you are proposing to visit. However, personal supplies of medicine are usually accepted worldwide.
- You should aim to keep your inhalers with you in the cabin rather than the hold of the aircraft. You may need to use them in a hurry. Some airlines carry their own emergency asthma treatment on some of their flights. If you use a spacer and can keep it with you well and good. If not, you can make an emergency one with a disposable coffee cup (see page 23). Take this ready-made with you; don't leave it to do on the aeroplane.
- As a rule, air travel does not present any problems for people with asthma but it is important to ensure that you sit far away from the smoking section. This is something you should be able to sort out with your travel agent and try and ensure that your aeroplane seat is booked in advance.
- If animal dander is a trigger for you, check that your hotel does not allow pets.
- Ask your travel agent to ensure that you are booked into a hotel that is regularly and thoroughly cleaned, particularly if dust mites are a problem. Ask for synthetic pillows and duvets and you may want to take a mattress cover with you. If you are travelling by car you may prefer to take your own pillows and duvet with you.
- When you get to your destination find out how and where you can get medical help if you need it. You will need to know where the nearest telephone is and you should make a note of the telephone number of a doctor or ambulance. Also find out where the nearest hospital casualty department is. The hotel staff or the local holiday representative should be able to provide you with all this information. If you are in a foreign country and cannot speak the language you also need to find out who could translate for you and where you can get hold of them in a hurry.

The *Holiday Care Service* gives information on holidays for people with disabilities. If you would like to get in touch with them their address is in Useful Addresses on page 149.

NAC/NES Joint Holiday Project

The National Asthma Campaign, in conjunction with the National Eczema Society, runs a series of holidays during the summer for different age groups. The idea is to bring young people together who have either asthma, eczema or both in a safe, happy environment where they can build up their confidence and social skills through doing a variety of activities.

Many of these activities are very adventurous and include sailing, canoeing, windsurfing, orienteering, fencing, archery, cycling, ice skating and dry-skiing. Everyone is encouraged to take part in and enjoy these pastimes knowing that there is medical and nursing support available round-the-clock. The idea is to help the holiday-makers put the condition to one side and get on with enjoying themselves in this vigorous and exciting way. It encourages people who may have limited their horizons because of their asthma to be more adventurous and take risks. In a controlled and caring atmosphere people are more likely to test limits because they know that if there are consequences there are professional carers to deal with them. It can have a very liberating effect.

Each holiday lasts a week and each week is closely supervised by a holiday leader who heads a team of helpers, many of whom have first hand experience of either asthma and/or eczema. In addition there are nurses and a doctor. Each holiday group comprises about 30 holiday-makers and about 15 to 18 helpers who are on hand 24 hours a day to provide encouragement, support and advice.

Emphasis is placed on health education and the medical staff run sessions on asthma and eczema and their practical management, including relaxation, breathing techniques, inhaler and medication use and the application of emollients and steroid creams. All the staff attend a training weekend to learn inhaler technique which they can then teach the youngsters in their care. All the medical equipment is set up to cope with asthma attacks and to look after the children whilst they are away from the centre. There are, of course, portable nebulisers to hand.

With such a large ratio of helpers to holiday makers, even the very young can be encouraged to try new activities and everyone can learn that they don't have to hide from life just because they have asthma. It may mean that they have to work a bit harder in looking after themselves, remembering to monitor their peak-flow daily and, of course, taking the inhalers regularly, but at the end of the day, they can usually do the same things as everybody else.

The holidays are divided into four age groups – children from six to nine and 10 to 13 and teenagers from 14 to 17. Ages for the young adult holiday-makers range from 18 to 25. The holidays are based in different centres and these are chosen for accommodation, situation and the friendliness of the staff. Accommodation is usually in four-bedded rooms with washing facilities. Everything is damp dusted. There are also ample bathing and showering facilities. A wide range of diets are anticipated and duly catered for.

On-site facilities usually include a swimming pool, gamesroom, craft rooms as well as meeting rooms and playing fields. All the grass in the area is cut before the holidaymakers arrive so as to reduce pollen levels. In addition to all the sports activities there are indoor activities like crafts, quizzes as well as talent shows, knock-out competitions and discos.

Although the emphasis is on fun and encouraging holiday-makers to try new activities, much attention is given to providing an atmosphere where people can get to know each other and talk about their condition without the fear of being misunderstood or stigmatised. Many young-sters find it easier to make friendships with members of the opposite sex in an environment where people understand the condition and the prob-lems it can produce. Many teenagers worry, for instance, about the intake of steroid tablets and the effect it can have on their appearance in terms, perhaps, of weight gain. It is often much easier to talk about these kinds of sensitive issues with people who can empathise from a personal standpoint rather than with even the most caring of listeners who hasn't had the experience first-hand.

One of the problems with teenagers who have asthma is that they don't like to be seen using their inhalers by people who do not have the condition. So non-compliance with treatments is a big factor with this age group. All ages can be tempted to give the daily treatment a miss when they are feeling fine. These kinds of issues are discussed in small informal groups where feelings and ideas can be safely aired. The impor-tance of keeping asthma in control with daily medication, if needed, is explained and emphasised.

Young adult holidays are planned on much the same lines where people can take part in the sports activities as and when they want to. However, many find it relaxing to be in the company of other people who have asthma or eczema and to be able to talk about their medication and problems in a way that they may not be able to do elsewhere.

The holidays are subsidised and some are grant-aided. If you would like to know about them contact the National Asthma Campaign or the National Eczema Society. Addresses of both organisations appear in the 'Useful Addresses' on page 149.

· *Exercise and sport* ·

The airways of people with asthma are constantly inflamed to a greater or lesser extent. Although the inflammation is ever-present, unless the condition is severe, this soreness may not be very noticeable until an irritant or allergic response increases the inflammation which causes the muscles in the airways to narrow, making the passage of air much more difficult. Amongst other things, exercise is a common asthma trigger. If after exercise you experience one or more of the following symptoms: breathlessness, wheezing, tight-chestedness or coughing you could be suffering from exercise-induced asthma.

If this is the case you can join the ranks of some very famous sportsmen – Olympic medallists to boot – and if it doesn't stop them, why should it stop you?

One of the most obvious signs of exercise-induced asthma is that you get the symptoms listed above within a minute of stopping the exercise. This is then followed by a worsening of the symptoms and the problems can last for up to half an hour. Some people only experience the asthma symptoms after exercise and are virtually unaware of the condition otherwise.

If you suspect you have exercise-induced asthma go and see your doctor and get it medically diagnosed. The doctor will do this by means of a peak-flow reading. If your peak-flow drops a few minutes after exercise, he or she will probably diagnose asthma. The doctor may then ask you to inhale a couple of puffs of a reliever inhaler. If this brings your peak-flow reading up, not only is the diagnosis of asthma confirmed, but the solution is also provided. Most athletes with exercise asthma find that taking one or two puffs of their reliever inhaler before sport, keeps them out of trouble. This may seem odd since normally the reliever treatment is only used when asthma symptoms occur, but in this instance it becomes a prophylactic.

Another medical option is to use *sodium cromoglycate* before sport. This is not a reliever but a preventer. It is a non-steroid anti-inflammatory medicine that can also work well with exercise-induced asthma. However *sodium cromoglycate* will not relieve the asthma symptoms once they have started.

Using these medicines should enable you to do most sport or exercise you want to do. You may find that there are some that don't suit. But you won't know until you try.

NB: *Scuba diving is one sport that is not recommended for people with asthma unless the condition is very mild and you haven't experienced wheezing in the last 48 hours. Something like parachuting which may involve the use of oxygen or pressurised air should not be contemplated without first seeking medical advice.*

There are some circumstances which are more likely to trigger exercise-induced asthma than others and it is worth knowing what these are.

● *Cold air* is one. Exercise taken outside on a cold, dry day is more likely to provoke an inflammation of the airways than exercise taken when the air is warm and moist. This is why swimming in an indoor pool is so beloved of asthma sufferers. The warm and moist atmosphere of an indoor swimming pool is unlikely to trigger an asthma attack unless the pool is heavily chlorinated. Chlorine can be a trigger for some people with asthma.

● *Long periods of exercise* are more likely to trigger asthma than short bursts. You are putting yourself at far more risk, for instance by, running a marathon than playing an hour's game of tennis. So a cross country run on a dry frosty day could be bad news while a game of football on a warm, moist evening should present much less of a problem.

● *Pollen* is another factor to consider. If pollen is a trigger for your asthma, obviously taking any exercise outside when the pollen count is high is going to put you in the target area for an attack.

● *Exercise with both arms and legs* is more likely to provoke an attack than just using one or the other.

One way of trying to prevent a possible attack is to exercise before doing any vigorous sport. A few 30-second sprints taken over 5-10 minutes can protect the lungs for an hour or so.

By the way, if you are planning on entering competitive sport and are worried about steroids please remember that the steroids you may be taking for asthma are *corticosteroids* and not *anabolic steroids* which are taken by some athletes to improve their performance. Inhaled steroids taken for asthma are usually allowed by sporting agencies. However, steroids taken in tablet form or injected may not be allowed. *Intal, Cromogen* and *Tilade* are also usually permitted as are *Ventolin* and *Bricanyl*. If you would like to know more contact the Sports Council's Doping Control Unit (see Useful Addresses page 149).

· *Pregnancy and breast-feeding* ·

Asthma in pregnancy varies a great deal from woman to woman. For some women the condition improves. With others it stays the same, and for a third group it can get worse. The absolute rule for every pregnant woman with asthma is that now more than ever you need to keep the condition under control. Virtually all the drugs taken by inhaler are safe to use in pregnancy. Uncontrolled asthma is not. Severe asthma attacks can reduce the amount of oxygen available to the foetus. This can result in the baby being born underweight.

Inhaling steroid preventer drugs like *beclomethasone, budesonide* and *fluticasone* is considered to be safe in pregnancy. The medicine acts in the lungs with very little getting into the bloodstream. It is through the bloodstream that the drugs can be passed from mother to baby. Equally, the non-steroid preventers *sodium cromoglycate* and *nedocromil* are safe for pregnant women as are the relievers *terbutaline* and *salbutamol. Aminophylline* tablets are also considered all right. If the drugs you are taking are not mentioned above please note this definitely does **not** mean that they are unsafe. Those listed are just given as examples. Check with your doctor that they are all right.

Women worry about taking medicine in pregnancy, and not without cause. But it is very important to bear in mind that severe asthma during pregnancy which reduces the levels of oxygen to the foetus can injure the unborn baby. Taking medication which is not considered to be harmful in pregnancy is the better option.

If you suffer from a severe form of the condition and are on steroid tablets, these are also permissible. Doses of up to 5mg per day are not considered harmful. If you need to take more than that it does not necessarily mean that it will harm the baby, but you do need to discuss your dosage with your doctor. If you are taking any steroid tablets at all during pregnancy, please keep your doctor informed.

Sometimes antibiotics will be needed to treat chest infections. Some, like *amoxycillin,* are considered safe whereas others, like *tetracycline,* are not prescribed for pregnant women.

Managing your asthma at this important period of your life is essential. Using a peak-flow meter and keeping a daily chart of your readings may be a bit of a hassle but it will pay off in terms of being in control. This way, if there seems to be a deterioration in the condition you can take early action. All it may require is an increase in the preventer medication.

Although avoiding triggers can be difficult, if not impossible at times, it does make sense to try and be extra careful to avoid an attack. If you smoke, now is the time to stop. Many women find that they do not crave cigarettes quite so much when they are pregnant, particularly in the early months if they are nauseous. Remember that if you smoke during pregnancy you are putting your baby at much greater risk of developing breathing problems and asthma. It also means that your baby may be born weighing less than he or she would do if you did not smoke. If you need help in giving up smoking telephone *Quitline.* The number is in Useful Addresses on page 149.

If you are worried about your asthma during labour, don't worry in silence, discuss it with your doctor or midwife. The National Asthma Campaign publish a useful leaflet on *Asthma and Pregnancy.* Although severe asthma attacks are rare during labour, it will help reassure you if *you* know that *they* know. Antenatal classes that teach breathing and relaxation exercises to use during labour are worth attending. Take your reliever inhaler before you start the exercises and this should obviate any symptoms of asthma.

Epidurals and normal painkillers used during labour are considered safe for asthma sufferers. However, if an operation is needed, it is important that the anaesthetist knows that you have asthma.

Most women are encouraged to breast-feed these days and there is nothing to prevent you from doing so. Breast-feeding is thought to guard against a baby developing atopic eczema and although the case for asthma is not so strong, if your family has a history of atopic conditions, it is a very good idea to give breast-feeding a serious go – if you can.

Again, the inhaled drugs will only be present in minuscule quantities in breast milk and so will provide no problem. If you are taking steroid inhalers and want to reduce the quantity entering the bloodstream even further, you can do this by using a spacer device – the *Volumatic* or *Nebuhaler*. (You can also do this during pregnancy if you want.) But really this is not a problem.

· *Asthma in the elderly* ·

It is estimated that 50 per cent of people who have asthma develop it before they are 10 years old. But it can appear at any age: Some 8 per cent of people diagnosed as having asthma are over the age of 65.

This age group can be difficult to diagnose. Many elderly people with asthma do not wheeze. The asthma may also accompany other lung conditions like chronic bronchitis or emphysema. Writing in the Autumn 1993 issue of *Asthma News,* Christopher Whipp explains: 'So, in order to test for asthma, doctors will administer an inhaled dose of reliever. In a person with asthma, this would result in the widening of previously narrow airways and the ability to breathe more easily. But not all elderly people with asthma will respond to the test. In some, the airways have become permanently narrow, and the constriction can only be partially reversed.'

Some elderly people, particularly if they have arthritis, may find the usual inhaler devices difficult to use. However, there are inhalers that have been devised with this type of user in mind which the doctor should be able to prescribe. Others may have difficulty in coordinating the inhaler at the same time as breathing in. In these cases the inhalers which automatically release the medicine on inhalation will overcome this problem.

An elderly person with asthma may well have other complaints needing treatment. Always make sure that anyone treating you for any other condition is aware of the fact that you have asthma as some drugs, used for other illnesses, can cause serious problems with asthma. Beta-blockers, for instance, used for treating high blood pressure or glaucoma should not be given to an asthma sufferer. These can bring on a severe, sometimes fatal, asthma attack. If you think you might be taking a beta-blocker, check with your doctor before stopping: you will need some other medicine instead. Aspirin can also present a problem as can some non-steroid anti-inflammatory painkillers. Please don't feel embarrassed about asking your doctor (or even your pharmacist) if you are at all worried about the medicine you have been prescribed. Your health is far more important.

· PATRICIA ·

When I was eight years old the War broke out and we were taken from my parents and put into a foster home. It was very traumatic. We didn't know if we would ever see them again. My father was working in a munitions factory and my mother was making gas masks. We were living in London near Putney Bridge and that's where they thought the Germans would bomb. They were right. Luckily we weren't there when the bomb was dropped on our home.

I was evacuated with my two sisters to a house in Reading. We were put in this home in the care of a so-called children's nurse. She abused us – not sexually but psychologically.

She went out of her way to be cruel and she terrified the life out of us. We used to sleep on camp beds and we had sleeping bags. In those days the sleeping bags didn't have zips, they had string on the top. She'd pull the sleeping bags over our heads and tie them up at the top. You felt as if you were suffocating.

I think that's where my nervousness comes from. I get asthma when I'm nervous or panicky.

She had no children of her own, this woman, and she got a great deal of enjoyment from bullying us. She would do all sorts of things. She'd lock us in the room. I never liked meat. She would buy pickled pork which was lumps of meat with lots of fat on it. She would put it on our plates and say we had to eat it. I'd put it in my mouth and I'd vomit it up. She was determined I was going to eat it so in the end she'd chop it up small and put it in my porridge the next morning. As fast as it went down, so it came up.

I don't know how long we were in that household. I know we were away from my parents for four years. My mother didn't know anything about what was going on. Every time my eldest sister wrote home to my mother the woman used to read the letter and make sure that there was nothing in it that would incriminate her. Eventually on a visit from my mother my sister was able to tell her what was happening. We were moved and this time we were with a very kind elderly lady.

I think all my nervousness stems from those days with that cruel woman.

I didn't have asthma as a child but I had eczema very badly. It wasn't the dry kind. It was very weepy and very nasty to look at. It always used to come up on my face and I didn't like to go out.

When I was older the doctor told me that when I got married the eczema would go away!

I got married when I was 24 years old. We went to Brighton for our honeymoon. I woke up at three o'clock one morning fighting for my breath. It scared the life out of my husband and he was a nurse. He took me out on to the balcony for fresh air and it helped. But I think it was nerves that brought it on. In those days things were different. You never lived together before you got married and you weren't naughty. Honeymoons could be quite testing.

That was my first asthma attack and I've had it ever since. As the years went on the eczema seemed to fade and the asthma got worse. As a child the eczema would come out in times of stress. Now it's the same with the asthma. I am very highly strung and I get excited over the slightest thing. As soon as I start getting uptight my chest tightens and I have difficulty in breathing.

My husband was a smoker. When we were first married he would be smoking over 40 a day. When we got the children and the mortgage he had to cut down. But at that time we didn't know that cigarettes were harmful or that they could trigger asthma. But I always found it an irritant. I'd tell my husband that the cigarettes were making me cough but he didn't believe me. He'd say there was nothing wrong with cigarettes and that people had been smoking for years.

His mother also smoked a lot. Sometimes when I would get wheezy she would tell my husband to give me a cigarette. She said it would help me cough it up. I once took a puff of a cigarette when I was feeling asthmatic and I coughed so much that I thought my face would burst. I found the taste of the cigarette disgusting.

I was in hospital once suffering with pneumonia. I was in a ward full of people with some form of lung disease. My husband came to visit me and he wanted to know what all these people were doing there. I told him they all had lung complaints mainly brought on by smoking. He made three attempts to give it up and succeeded a few years before he died. But sadly it was too late for him. He died of a massive heart attack at the age of 59.

Thank goodness none of my three children smoke. My son had asthma as a child but he doesn't have it now.

I think one of my other problems was diesel fumes. When the children were born we bought a house on a main road on top of a hill. The buses would be going backwards and forwards all day and they'd rev up the hill. You'd open the windows for fresh air but what you were actually getting was diesel fumes. I don't think it helped my lungs much.

My asthma is not bad, but I have to take daily medication. I take Becotide twice a day and Ventolin when I need it. If I get a cold it goes straight to my chest. I'm also very allergic to feathers. All my bedding is synthetic and I use those special liners. I find they help a lot. But the main thing that sets off my asthma is nerves. My sister says I have to calm down. I must learn to relax. But I've always been a highly strung person. That's the way I am.

SHEILA

From the age of 19 I had allergic rhinitis. I sniffed constantly. In fact I had a reputation amongst my friends as being someone who sniffed. When I became pregnant with my first child it got very bad, so much so that I felt I couldn't breathe. They introduced me to a spray which cleared it for a few hours at a time. It was really quite good.

A few years later I was introduced to the Beconase spray which totally transformed my life. There would be times when I would try stopping the Beconase to see what would happen, but after a couple of months I'd have to go back on it. That's how it was until the summer of 1993.

In 1992 my daughter and I decided to buy a couple of little kittens. They were gorgeous. About nine or 10 months later I started getting asthma symptoms. Out of the blue I developed a cough. It wasn't just an ordinary cough. It felt as if it was a permanent itch or tickle down my throat and it got progressively worse.

It began to interfere with my life. I couldn't go on a train journey without a bottle of water and things to suck. I was frightened of going to the cinema or theatre in case I started coughing. In the end I wasn't sure if I was becoming nervous about coughing, but the whole thing just took over.

This started in the May and I waited until early August before I went to the surgery. The doctor listened to my chest and I breathed into something and he said to me that he felt I was asthmatic. He wasn't totally sure. He put me on a short course of steroids. He wanted to see what my reaction would be to the tablets. They started to work pretty quickly and within two days it had started to noticeably improve.

I went back to the surgery the following week and the doctor said that I had asthma. He started me on inhaled steroid, two puffs twice a day and he said that it would keep everything at bay. This is exactly what I've been doing ever since. And I've discovered that if I exhale the Becotide through my nose I don't need to use the Beconase. So I don't take that any more.

I have twice decided I was better and taken myself off the Becotide, but both times after a while the symptoms started up again. So I put myself back on to it.

I am not a wheezy person. I don't get tight-chested. I just get this strange cough. If I get a cold it goes straight into this cough which is far more troublesome than the cold.

I don't know if the cats triggered the asthma. My father has asthma so it's in the family and I know I am allergic to cats. When the friendly one, Mitzi, comes and sits next to me my eyes start to sting quite badly. It's very uncomfortable.

· JANICE ·

My asthma was a late onset. I was 50 years old. I was suffering from a bad cough and I was in a very stressful job at the time. I had been given Benylin and Codeine for the cough. We were going to live in another part of Europe because of my husband's job. Normally I would take this in my stride because I am so used to moving, I could do it standing on my head. But this time I was desperately worried. I was leaving everything familiar and I wasn't well. I felt I was an impediment rather than an asset. Emotionally I was in a state.

Shortly after we moved, the Benylin and Codeine mixture ran out and I couldn't get any more. So I bought some Benylin over the counter. It seemed to be having the strange effect of constricting my throat but I persisted with it because I wanted to keep the cough at bay. However I woke up at three o'clock one morning with a severe asthma attack. I was taken into hospital where I stayed for a week. I was diagnosed as having asthma which shook me rigid. My mother had asthma but up until then I'd shown no signs of it. I'd been extremely fit all my life. The asthma attack was a turning point in my life. Nothing like that had happened to me before that.

Along with the asthma it was discovered that I had allergic rhinitis. Eventually I was put on Beconase for the rhinitis and Becotide and Ventolin for the asthma.

Everything was more or less under control with occasional flare-ups of rhinitis or asthma until eight years later. I was back in England and helping out in a barn when somebody shook a very old and dusty carpet near me. It had a devastating effect. It set off my asthma but it did far worse things to my nose which was continually blocked after that. In fact the rhinitis gave me far more trouble than the asthma at that time.

After the dust episode I developed thrush in my mouth. It was probably due to the steroids. I had been taking the Beconase solidly for eight years. I took myself off it when I didn't react particularly well to the anti-fungal treatment and every time I ate anything sugary it would aggravate the thrush. But it did eventually diminish.

Since then I have been very allergic to dust. Even now I have to wear a mask when I clean the house. I'm also allergic to mould spores.

I was producing a lot of mucus which might have been manageable except for the fact that I had developed nasal polyps. This meant that I couldn't blow my nose, so the mucus would go to my chest which was no good for my asthma.

The asthma is such that I don't have attacks but I get short-winded in dif-ferent situations and environments. I've always been very active and still am, but I can no longer do things like play tennis because I just haven't got the lung capacity. I can't handle smoky places. Cold weather affects me. If it's very cold and I walk down to the shops I can get short-winded. I have to slow down my pace and take my Ventolin. But, equally, if I go from a cold to a warm environment that can make me feel breathless. In the winter I can be taking Ventolin as much as six or seven times a day. In the summer it's not so bad. When I'm gardening I can have problems but I rarely take the Ventolin more than four times a day during the summer months.

I have recently had the nasal polyps removed. It's changed my life. I can sleep. I'm breathing a lot better and I can blow my nose. I feel like a new person. I still have to watch my asthma of course. But I can control it. I see my doctor about once every six weeks. He keeps an eye on me but on a day-to-day basis it's in my hands now.

I take a peak-flow reading every day, night and morning. As soon as I wake up the first thing I do is to take a puff of Ventolin. Then I go and have breakfast. Sometimes after breakfast I may need another puff of Ventolin. Then I check my peak-flow. So I take the reading after taking Ventolin. If my asthma is stable it will be around 270 litres per minute. I think if I was doing it before the Ventolin it would be around 230. Anyway, if it's around 270 post Ventolin I'm quite happy. If it drops below 250 for more than two days I know I'm on a downhill path. I then put myself on oral steroids (Prednisolone 5ml) for a few days. That stabilises me. Before I had my polyps removed I could be taking as many as 200-280 Prednisolone tablets a year – not so much for the asthma, but to unblock my nose. I don't take anything like that amount now.

I don't find asthma an impediment at all now. I can control it. I can do virtually everything I want to do – I just have to keep tabs on the condition.

9

BABIES AND CHILDREN

It is estimated that in the United Kingdom at least one child in every seven is diagnosed as having asthma. Asthma is one of the most common chronic diseases in the Western world and the number of children diagnosed with it is increasing. Ten per cent of all school children are likely to miss classes because they have asthma. Why this illness is on the rise is not known. As far as children are concerned parental smoking, viruses, low birth weight and pollution are some of the possible causes currently being examined. Parental smoking has been proven to increase the likelihood of a child having asthma. If the mother smokes during pregnancy or either parent smokes during the child's early years, the latter stands a much greater chance of developing asthma.

Unfortunately , not everyone who has asthma as a child grows out of it. Young children whose asthma is mild have a 60–80 per cent chance of losing their symptoms during their teens. But those with a more severe form of the illness are more likely to continue into adulthood. Even those people whose symptoms disappear for years on end can suddenly find that some time in their adult life, asthma is back on the menu. But for about one in three children asthma disappears forever.

Childhood asthma terrifies parents. My own child has asthma, thankfully in a mild form. Even so there have been a few late-night or early-morning dashes to the hospital as well as, of course, urgent calls to the doctor. Probably the worst experience was the one laden with guilt. I allowed her to sleep in a cigarette smoke-filled room, assuming it would be all right since no one was smoking at the time. The smoke that remained in the room triggered her asthma and she spent a very uncomfortable night in a nearby hospital gasping for breath. It was far from all right.

After that my anxiousness went into over-drive and I worried about everything – especially if she was invited to sleep at a friend's house. Was there a cat in the house? Did the family smoke? Would she be sleeping on the floor or on a bed? Were there feather pillows? Did the parental IQ run to calling an ambulance? Of course all these questions, apart from the last one, were valid, but to be allowed to have a normal childhood is not an unreasonable request. So we eventually arrived at a compromise whereby she was allowed to sleep at friends' houses so long as there were no cats or cigarettes and she took her own sleeping bag and pillows. And, of course, her inhalers.

Obviously, the rules are going to vary according to the severity of the child's asthma. At any level it is a juggling act. Asthma is a serious condition and attacks can be dangerous or even fatal. So you have every right to worry. But against this you have to balance the child's need to have friends and do most, if not all, of the things that other children do. It is very important for your child to feel that he or she is the same as any other. This can sometimes be difficult to achieve but children hate feeling different and it can make them isolated and lonely. The psychological aspect of the condition really does need consideration. An unhappy child is a stressed one and this can have a detrimental effect on the condition.

Parental guilt is another factor. Whatever chronic illness a child might have – be it asthma, eczema, migraine, colitis, psoriasis and so on – parents often feel that they are to blame. They did or are doing something wrong. If you have read Chapter 1 you will know that a predisposition to asthma is inherited. Along with your good looks, intelligence, creative abilities, and captivating smile, your child has inherited the possibility of having asthma. You may be shaking your head and saying vehemently; 'Not me – it's not in my family.' And your spouse may be saying the same thing.

Generally speaking, asthma that appears in childhood is atopic asthma. It is thought that as many as a third of all people would prove to be atopic if tested. So somewhere in your child's family tree is at least one relative with at least one of the atopic conditions and these are asthma, eczema, allergic rhinitis and hayfever. By no means everyone who is atopic suffers with these illnesses, but a predisposition to them exists. With a third of the population in the atopic frame it is quite possible that a tendency for asthma is present in both your families – yours and your partner's. It just may never have appeared as asthma before but as another of the atopic conditions already mentioned.

So forget the guilt and concentrate on a positive approach. Please read the other chapters in this book. The chapter on triggers is very relevant to childhood asthma as are all the other chapters with the exception of Chapter 7.

Get to know as much as you can about the condition and try and explain it to your child. Let him understand that asthma isn't the result of something he (or she) has done wrong. It is just a part of who he is. Try and explain the difference between the preventer and reliever treatments and between the two of you try to discover, as best you can, which are the triggers. Obviously how much of this you can do will depend on the age of your child, but the more he understands the more confident he will be of his ability to cope. As he (or she) grows older he will be out and about on his own more and more, going on school trips or unsupervised outings with friends. The sooner he can take at least some of the responsibility for his condition, the more he will be able to take these things in his stride.

· *The under-fives* ·

It can be difficult to diagnose asthma in a very young child. First of all, 30 per cent of all under-five-year-old children experience at least one period of wheezing. Most of these will not go on to have asthma. Second, the peak-flow meter which is so useful in diagnosing asthma in adults and older children is not effective in children under the age of about six. So what are the telltale signs? The following are suggested by the National Asthma Campaign:

- Repeated attacks of wheezing and coughing, usually with colds.
- A cough that won't go away or keeps coming back.
- Restless nights due to wheezing and/or coughing.
- Wheezing and/or coughing between colds, especially after exercise or excitement, or on exposure to cigarette smoke and allergic triggers such as dust, pets, pollens or feathers.

A persistent dry and irritating cough may be the only symptom of asthma. The cough can produce phlegm and be so violent that it makes them sick. Children without asthma do not cough in this way – coughing for them is usually accompanied by a cold.

Triggers

Triggers in this age group are similar to those at any age and it is worth reading Chapter 5 to get ideas about these.

- **Cigarette smoke** is particularly harmful to all young lungs, let alone the lungs of young children with asthma. Please keep your child away from smoky areas and if you or your partner smoke please do so away from your child and out of the house. Also bear in mind that a woman who smokes during pregnancy passes on a greater risk of asthma to her child.

Other common triggers in this age group include the following:

- Colds and viruses are very difficult to avoid and they are a very common trigger for this age group. If your baby is likely to be allergic, it is recommended that you breast-feed for as long as you can as it may offer some protection.

However, it is very likely that your child will catch colds from time to time. Make sure you know how to deal with the asthma that may ensue. Talk to your doctor and make sure you have an adequate supply of preventers and relievers and you know how to use them. These are explained more fully later in this chapter.

● Some children are sensitive to cold air and may wheeze or cough when they go out on a cold day. However, children do need to be able to go outside, so wrap them up warmly and you may find that a puff of the reliever inhaler taken just before going out will obviate any breathing problems.

● House dust mites, pets, pollen and exercise are some of the other common triggers for children of all ages, and these are discussed briefly further on in this chapter and in more detail in Chapter 5.

Treatment

If you have read Chapter 2 you will know that asthma treatment is based on two types of drugs: those that protect the airways and so work to prevent an attack from happening and those that open up the constricted airways and in so doing treat the attack and bring 'relief'. The first type of drugs are known as **preventers** and the second as **relievers.** Incidentally, dosage of inhaled drugs can sometimes be higher for young children than for adults. This is because they are not so good at inhaling the drug and a very small proportion of the medicine reaches the lungs.

A commonly used preventer for children is *sodium cromoglycate*. This is a non-steroid, anti-inflammatory drug. If you find that your child is using the reliever inhaler (explained next) more than once a day you should ask your doctor if your child needs some kind of preventer treatment.

If this form of preventer does not work, the doctor may prescribe a low-dose steroid inhaler. With young children these are usually inhaled through a spacer (described below) and since the dosage is so tiny these steroids do not cause side-effects.

Preventer treatment has to be taken regularly, as prescribed, whether the asthma is apparent or not. It is not designed to treat attacks. This is the job of the reliever medicine.

Relievers relax the tiny muscles in the airways which dilates them and makes breathing easier. They are usually used when symptoms appear but can also be used to protect against triggers like exercise and cold air if used just before the event. For children under the age of 12 months, finding the right reliever can be a matter of trial and error. Not all of them work well for that age group, so if you find the that the one that has been prescribed for your child is not having the desired effect, go back and see your doctor. It is very important that you get the right drug. The most commonly used relievers are *salbutamol* and *terbutaline*. For some children *Atrovent* (*ipratropium*) is more helpful.

The most effective way of treating asthma is through inhalers because it gets the drug straight to the place where it is needed. There are a variety of inhalers available. Some are aerosols (puffers) and these look like miniature spray cans. Others are dry powder inhalers. *Turbohaler, Diskhaler* or *Spinhaler* are three dry-powder inhalers which are often prescribed to children over the age of three. However, when a child is wheezy or tight chested they will find using a dry powder inhaler very difficult and in these cases an aerosol inhaler is preferable.

All children under the age of four need a spacer to fit their aerosol inhaler, together with a face mask. These make it possible for this age group to inhale the medicine. Older children are usually able to manage without the mask.

Children with severe asthma can sometimes be prescribed a nebuliser for extra help in taking their medicine. But generally speaking spacers are considered to be equally efficacious.

It can be difficult to get young children to take inhaled medicine and so they are sometimes prescribed bronchodilators in syrup form. However here are some tips you might like to try when giving inhaled medicine to your child:

● Get babies used to the feel of a mask by stroking their cheek with it.
● Don't worry if your baby cries. Keep the mask over his face as he will breathe in after crying.
● If your baby pushes the spacer away from his mouth, gently wrap his arms around his chest.
● You can use the spacer on babies and young children while they are asleep. You can do this by holding the spacer and mask over the child's face while he sleeps. He will breathe in the treatment.
● Try, if you can, to make a game of the routine. You can decorate the spacer and puffer to look like a toy. You can show your child how to use it by demonstrating it on yourself, but don't fire the puffer. If you can possibly make it fun rather than intense you will communicate that feeling to your child.
● Give him (or her) the medication even if he is crying, because he will still breathe it in. Try not to waste time in pleading, give the drug as quickly as possible and this should calm things down.

If your child has asthma and is coughing a lot please don't give him (or her) cough syrup unless the doctor specifically tells you to. Cough syrup very rarely helps a child with asthma but may instead make matters worse by creating a sticky phlegm which blocks the air passages.

Handling an attack

During an asthma attack wheezing and coughing can worsen very quickly to the extent that the child becomes too short of breath to speak.

Other signs of a serious attack are when the child is very pale or quiet; if he or she lies very still or if he or she is breathing very fast; and also if the lips are blue.

Obviously this can be very traumatic for parents so it is as well to have a plan of action up your sleeve. Attacks can come on quite suddenly or take days to build up. In any event you need to discuss what to do with your doctor. Make sure you understand the plan thoroughly and write it down. When we are very worried we often forget things that we normally know very well. Keep your notes handy and in the same place all the time. The emergency plan you work out with your doctor is unlikely to be complicated. It may very well be along the lines suggested by the National Asthma Campaign:

● Give your child the reliever treatment immediately, wait five to 10 minutes and repeat until breathing improves or until help arrives. Give your child steroid tablets if they have been prescribed by your doctor.
● Hold or sit the child in an upright position to assist breathing. Some mothers say that if they have a small child who is having an attack they will sit him (or her) on their knee and put the child's arms on the mother's neck. This way the child is being cuddled and comforted but the chest is kept expanded.
● Call your doctor or an ambulance (whichever is quicker in your area) or take your child to the nearest hospital.

If your child goes to hospital always make a follow-up appointment either with the hospital or with your GP. You may need to discuss with your doctor the possible reasons for the attack. It is important to keep a regular check on your child's condition. Signs of deterioration are:

● Increase in the use of the reliever medicine.
● Coughing or wheezing first thing in the morning.
● Night time coughing or wheezing.
● Increase in wheezing or coughing after exercise.

If your child's asthma is deteriorating, tell your doctor. You may need to increase or change the preventer treatment.

Childcare

Finding the right kind of childcare for any working parent can be fraught with difficulty, but for the parents of a child with asthma there are special considerations. The trigger factor is an important one and you will need to know if your child is going to be in a smoky atmosphere. Are there pets around? Is it very dusty? These are the kind of possible triggers to look out for as well as, of course, any other specific ones that are known to you.

In addition, you will need to be sure that the people looking after your child will know what to do in an emergency. Do they know about asthma? Would they be able to handle an attack? Would they contact you immediately?

It is important to give your child's carers clear written instructions of any medication that needs to be taken as well as details of any emergency plan you have worked out with your doctor.

The National Asthma Campaign produces a *School Card* which can be used for pre-school children in nurseries. The card is filled in by your doctor and sets out which medication the child needs to take and when to take it. It also gives instructions of what needs to be done in an emergency. Please try and ensure that your childminder, nursery, or play group is registered with the local authority. The National Asthma Campaign has a video about asthma suitable for those who look after school children and pre-school children. It is available from the head office.

· *Older children* ·

Recognising asthma in older children is very similar to diagnosing it in adults. This being the case, please read Chapter 1 which details the symptoms. It also helps you to assess the severity of the illness in your child. But to recap, some indications of the condition are:

● **Breathlessness.** If your child gets short of breath much more quickly than others and is sometimes breathless, this could be a sign of asthma.
● **Tight chest.** A cold or flu can leave anyone feeling tight chested but asthma people can experience this even when they haven't had a virus. Also if your child takes longer than others to get over viruses and inevitably needs extra treatment, he or she could have asthma.
● **Wheezing** is an indication of asthma.
● **Coughing that is recurrent** and may produce a yellow, green or white mucus can be an indication of asthma, particularly if it is accompanied by wheezing.
● **Cold air** is a trigger for many people with asthma and causes them to be breathless, wheezy or cough a lot.

As with adults there are two other ways in which doctors diagnose asthma in children. One is to give patients anti-asthma medicine but with children over the age of six a quicker and more accurate method is by means of a peak-flow meter.

Peak-flow meters are not only a very important diagnostic tool, they are also extremely valuable to use every day to keep a check on your child's condition. Unless your child's asthma is very mild, you should ask for a peak-flow meter, which is available on prescription, to use at home as part of an asthma management plan. More about peak-flow meters appears in Chapter 3.

Triggers

As has been discussed, people with asthma have particularly sensitive airways in their lungs. Obviously if your child can avoid the things that cause inflammation it is better than taking drugs. Although it is very unlikely that you will be able to achieve this it is possible to cut down on some of the irritants and allergens which adversely affect your child. In this way you can minimise the intake of medicine. Cigarette smoke has already been mentioned early on in this chapter. Passive smoking is particularly hazardous for a child with asthma and is something that can be avoided to a very large extent. Please read Chapter 5 on triggers detailing those which are indicated in asthma. Here, as a quick guide, are some that are prevalent in children with asthma.

● **House dust mites** are a common trigger in everyone with asthma, young children included.
● **Pets** are another major trigger for asthma. You do have to take into consideration that pets can make the condition very much worse for many, if not most, sufferers.
● **Viruses,** particularly colds and flu, almost inevitably cause problems for people with asthma. Anti-flu injections, given annually, are available from your GP and people with asthma are given priority treatment. Ask your doctor if he or she thinks your child should have an anti-flu injection. These are not usually given to very young children.
● **Pollen** can be a difficult trigger to avoid, particularly for children who will naturally want to play outside. Grass pollen probably presents the worst problem and if your child is affected by pollen between early May and the end of July it is probably grass pollen he or she is reacting to. Trees pollinate between the beginning of April and the end of May.
● **Sport**, particularly running, can produce symptoms in children with asthma. It is usually at its worst a few minutes after the exercise. Funnily enough, for some people the asthma improves if they keep on with the exercise. The symptoms subside. This is because vigorous exercise increases the level of adrenaline in the blood stream and adrenaline dilates the airways. But it doesn't work for everybody. Asthma that comes on during exercise could have a variety of causes, cold air and pollen being two.

Taking sodium cromoglycate can help to prevent exercise- induced asthma or you may find that a dose of the reliever inhaler taken before the exercise may obviate the problem. However, both these possible treatments should be discussed with your GP or asthma nurse before offering them to your child. Warming-up before a sporting activity is also a good preventative measure. Several 30-second sprints over a period of five to 10 minutes before the sport can protect the lungs for about an hour.

Although exercising the whole body is more likely to bring on an asthma attack than exercising arms or legs alone, sport and exercise are very important to your child so please don't be tempted to curtail this activity. Children produce growth hormone when exercising which is one reason why it is such an important part of their lives. They also produce this hormone during sleep.

Not only does it build their bodies and strength, exercise – especially vigorous exercise – is excellent for releasing stress. Children today can have a lot of stress from school work and exams, and they do need an outlet. Remember, too, that some of our best sportsmen have asthma so there must be a way of coping for most people.

Swimming is a sport which seems to attract the least problems for people with asthma and the reasons why are discussed in Chapter 5.

If sporting activities are a problem for your child talk to your doctor about it. Don't be afraid of 'wasting his time'. It is a very important issue and GPs are paid to help you sort out problems like this.

The one sport that people with asthma may need to avoid is scuba diving which can be dangerous for all but those with the mildest asthma.

● **Cold air** can be an asthma trigger particularly if the air is dry as well. Cold air cools the airways and can make them dry and twitchy. Going from a warm house into the cold air outside can pose a special problem with wheezing and coughing. If it is a cold dry day, try giving your child an extra dose of reliever treatment before he or she goes out.

● **Weather** can be a factor for some people with asthma. A sudden change in the temperature can trigger wheezing. Just as going from a warm house into the cold air triggers wheezing, so can going from cool to warm or very hot weather. Although the humidity surrounding a swimming pool is usually favourable to asthma sufferers, humidity in the weather can pose problems. This may be due to an allergy to the moulds that accompany humid conditions rather than the weather itself. Similarly, high winds and thunderstorms can release pollens into the atmosphere which can cause sensitivity in some people. On the other hand, people who are allergic to grass pollen will be more susceptible in dry weather when the pollen count is higher.

● **Laughing** unfortunately, can often make people wheeze. This is probably caused by the sharp intake of breath which can dry out the airways. Treatment for this is similar to that of exercise-induced asthma.

· *The parents* ·

Parenting a child who has a chronic condition, particularly if it is severe, must be one of the most difficult situations in life. The open-ended commitment and constant care required by a child with these kinds of needs can place a very large burden on the parents and often the entire family is held hostage – at least for a while. Tiredness through lack of sleep is a common problem and one that can make it very difficult to look at things from a positive perspective. One mother told me that she cannot remember when she last had a good night's sleep. Her child is 10 years old and was diagnosed with asthma when he was two. Although his asthma is now reasonably well managed, the sudden night-time attacks that used to take place have left her feeling very anxious. She fears that he will have an attack in the night and worries that she won't hear him. So she seldom relaxes enough to sleep deeply and most of the time does little more than catnap through the night.

The father of a 15-year-old girl whose asthma is now in remission said that he could not believe the change in the household since his daughter's condition has disappeared. 'When I look back at us a couple of years ago it is like a different lifetime and another family. Somehow the flashbacks seem to be in black and white – there's that greyness to those times. I suppose now we have the time and the energy to have fun.'

One mother whose child has brittle asthma gave up a challenging and lucrative career because she could not combine it with looking after her daughter. Even her social life has had to be severely curtailed.

Although the main focus of this book is to look at asthma from a positive perspective, I believe that it is important also to acknowledge the problems it creates. Asthma can be a very difficult condition to handle. Along with the practicalities of keeping it under control and dealing with attacks when they arise are the emotional and psychological elements. It is hard for parents who are exhausted, anxious and constantly on the watch for signs of deterioration in the condition of their asthmatic child, to respond to the needs of their other, more healthy children. As parents, we know that all our children need our affection and attention – not just the child who is ill. But as worried and tired human beings we cannot always find the energy to handle family life the way we would like. Yet it is important to try.

If you find that things are getting on top of you it might be worth considering short term counselling. Talking to a professional listener can often help you see the current situation from a different perspective. As the parent of a child with asthma you may have long forgotten to respect your own needs and allow yourself to do some of the things you want. Many parents of children who need attention over and above the norm say that they have had to put their lives 'on hold'. Counselling may help you address this. Chapter 13 describes the process of counselling in a little more detail.

The following is an account of living with asthma told from a parent's point of view. The child in question has a severe form of the illness.

· A Mother's story ·

My daughter was three when she was first diagnosed with asthma. It came out of the blue. She was coughing and wheezing and couldn't breathe. The doctor could not stabilise her and she was rushed off to hospital. The worst bit was when they put her on the drip. That was when I finally burst into tears. I could hear her screaming in the room where they do the nasties. They were trying to put the drip in and she was wriggling. She was too little to know what was going on. Having had my little weep I realised I had to be the sensible one and put on a brave face. At the time I didn't realise that this was something that was going to go on and on.

She has been asthmatic ever since. It wasn't too bad in the early years. Between the ages of six and eight she was in hospital every two months. By the time she was 10 years old she was on all the puffers as well as, from time to time, the oral steroids.

They said she would grow out of it at puberty but it got worse. She is 15 years old and her asthma is still severe. I have to be around all the time. It has impeded my career. I don't even relax when she goes off to school. I wonder if she is going to be all right, particularly if she is not a 100 per cent when she leaves. We have an understanding now that she is in charge of her asthma. She knows how she feels and she does the peak-flow every morning and she's a sensible girl. But sometimes she leaves for school looking ill and I'm constantly on edge, worrying about her. I'm jittery when the phone goes. Is it the school? Is she in an ambulance? What's happening to her?

We've had so many dramas. I've been in the ambulance when they've said to the driver 'Put your foot down mate' and said to me: 'the hospital is only just around the corner'. It's very scary.

When she was little I was running a busy office and I had a lot of help in the house but I couldn't combine the two. I couldn't get the worry of my daughter out of my mind and I couldn't be sure that the people who were looking after her were going to do it well. Was the action going to be swift enough? You only have so many breaths left. I started to get ill and I gave up work.

It's a bit like having a baby. You're always alert. I haven't been able to sleep properly for so long. Part of me is listening all the time. Sometimes there is a feeling that the other members of the family are left out. You have this special relationship and it appears that one person is getting more attention. You have to think very logically and try and give time to the others and also play the illness down. But it's a strain because you are putting up a front all the time and when you're exhausted it's difficult to pretend that you're fine.

It has taken over my life. Even though she's older she still needs care when she comes out of hospital. She needs to have nourishing food to build up her strength after an attack and I have to make sure that her peak-flow is normal before she goes back to school. I have to go on all the school trips with her. If anything happens I can whizz off with her in an ambulance.

We've not gone on holiday at all. The only holidays she's had are the ones arranged by the National Asthma Campaign. She's been two years running and she loves them. The only time I've been able to unwind is during those two weeks in those two years.

I think on of the biggest scares I've had was when we were out for drinks with friends one lunchtime. She was tugging at me trying to speak and I was saying, 'In a minute, darling.' I didn't realise that she was passed the point of being able to say what was wrong with her. I suddenly twigged what was happening and we rushed her to the hospital. That was a scary journey. Since then I have become more attuned. Normally when children are tugging at you it is not for anything important, but she was trying to tell me that she couldn't breathe any more and she didn't want everybody to know. Now when she makes any sign that she is bad I know that it's not a joke. She's never ever put it on. In fact she tends to minimise it.

But it is not all negative. The plus side is that it has created a very strong bond between us. We are very close. I don't feel that I have wasted my time as a human being. It puts a lot of other things into perspective and I don't resent it. Other people may tell me that I am wasting my talents but I feel that as long as I can get my daughter through, it doesn't matter.

It's not the life that I had mapped out in my head. I live a different sort of life from a lot of people in that I don't keep a diary. I keep as many days free as possible. Whenever I make an arrangement I always preface it by saying, 'you do understand that I might have to break this date because. . .'

We have spent so many hours, days and weeks together. It's more than the usual mother and daughter relationship. She knows my weaknesses and I know hers. I think that many of these severe asthmatics are able to cope with problems in their lives that other people may not be able to. I think it makes them stronger. She understands suffering, but she is not morbid about it. She will do something practical about it. She's the agony aunt around here. The telephone never stops. She has lots of friends and they're very supportive. They all know how to use the nebuliser.

She's always busy. She does modern dancing and tap and sometimes that will bring on the asthma. But she loves it. She's been in a few shows where she's become asthmatic during the performance but she's had the nebuliser and carried on. I think it's important for them to do as much as they can. It doesn't help to wrap them up. You have to keep a beady eye out for them, but you can't keep saying you can't do this or that. I've negotiated with my daughter what is sensible and what would be foolhardy.

When she was 14 years old my daughter was going to be confirmed. I decided I wanted to be confirmed with her. I had thought about it a lot and I felt it would help me spiritually. I took it very seriously and we were confirmed together. It has been a comfort. It was a very important day in my private and *spiritual life. I don't think I would have done it had it not been for the asthma. You get so desperately worried and upset that you look for things that will help. This has been another dimension. It has affirmed a point that I was coming to anyway which is to accept what is happening and live with it. I've never felt bitter. I believe that the main thing is to take each day as it comes and be grateful for the good bits.*

· KEITH AND CLIVE ·

Keith, aged 10, has asthma as does his brother Clive who is seven years old. The condition in both boys is well managed and both have it to more or less the same degree. However, each boy responds to the condition in a different way. They have a sister who does not have asthma. Their mother tells their story.

Clive was six months old when he was diagnosed as being asthmatic. He had been having a lot of chest complaints and he couldn't sleep properly. My husband and I would take it in turns to sit in bed with him. As soon as he went to sleep we'd try and lie him down in the bed but as soon as his body was flat he couldn't breathe and he would start choking again. This went on for about a year. As soon as he had a cold his asthma got really bad.

When he was able to move around he got a lot better. He's not too bad now until he gets a cold. He is blocked up a lot of the time but he doesn't take much notice of it. He thinks it is just part of life and takes it for granted.

The cold air affects him and he doesn't feel like being outside. He prefers to stay in and do his drawings. But he gets on well with the other kids and he is fine at school. He takes his inhalers at dinner time. He takes them through a spacer.

Clive has never been to hospital with an attack. He copes quite well during one and doesn't panic. The only thing that seems to worry him is being away from home. He doesn't like going on holiday. We've been going to Cornwall every year and his asthma usually gets worse when we get there. We normally spend a morning at the doctor's. I think they've got to know us down there!

Keith was diagnosed with asthma when he was five years old. He'd been poorly before that but we didn't know what it was. He'd had chest infection after chest infection. At school the teacher said that he didn't run around with all the other children. I now think the reason was that he couldn't – he got too breathless.

He has only been in hospital with an attack once. He had a cold which got worse and worse. The doctor who came to see him couldn't do anything with him. He kept putting the mask across his face and Keith didn't like that at all. He panicked. We're near a hospital and we took him there by car. They gave him oxygen and kept him in all night and stabilised him. Like Clive, he's on preventer and reliever treatment.

He is now a very active boy. He likes to swim and run. He is probably better at sport than a lot of his friends because he is more determined. He likes to win and he won't give in to the asthma. He plays football and has started running at the Exeter Harriers' track. He plays squash and golf. He has a hand in most sport and is quite good at all of them. There have been a couple of football matches he hasn't played in because he has not felt well. With running, squash or golf you can stop but with a team game like football it is more difficult to stop in the middle and say you're not feeling well. If he's going to do anything strenuous he has a puff of Ventolin beforehand.

We can usually tell when the boys are not well. Keith doesn't like to be told he can't do any sport because he's wheezy or short of breath but he normally admits it. We also check it out on the peak-flow meter. We know what a good reading is and if Keith wants to do some sport and we're worried about it, he goes on the peak-flow and we can tell whether he is well or not. He can see for himself how well he is. At 10 years old he has come to terms with when he can or can't do things.

A lot of Keith's asthma is due to stress and panic. If he's going back to school after a break he'll be bad because he will be worried about school.

We consider how the boys feel before we do anything. It has an effect on my daughter because often there are times when we don't do things because of the boys. She would like a dog or a cat. You can't have one for a week and send it back. They've been in contact with pets and been all right but it's only been for a short time. It's different when it's in your house. We've got a goldfish but it's not the same. It can be difficult to say no to a pet but she's come to terms with the fact that she's not having one. The boys are not that fussed. There was a cat up the road and once when Clive was walking down the path, the cat just came out in front of him and he tripped over it. He's disliked cats ever since!

· JACK ·

This little boy is now aged six. His mother tells his story:

When Jack was three months old he got eczema quite badly but it wasn't until he was nearly three years old that he developed asthma as well.

It started with a cold that went to his chest. When the doctor listened to his chest he said he thought Jack might be asthmatic. But it all cleared up quite quickly.

His first attack came about six months later. I had no idea what was wrong with him. He had a bad cold and he was very miserable and tired. I'd taken him to work with me because he wasn't well enough to take to the nursery. A colleague of mine whose children have also had asthma told me I should take him to the doctor. His chest was heaving and he seemed to be lifting his shoulders to breathe. I had no idea what was wrong but I knew he was poorly. He was walking around and he wasn't complaining. He was obviously very tired but I thought it was because of the infection. When I think about it now I want to cry.

The doctor said I had to take Jack to hospital right away. I couldn't believe it. He'd obviously had the asthma for two days and I hadn't recognised it.

They put him on steroids while he was in hospital which was for about 48 hours. After that he was fine. His temperature was down and his breathing was back to normal.

He went onto daily inhalers. He found the straightforward puffers very difficult. He then had a spacer which again he found difficult, but we persevered with that and he was able to do it daily. Over the next two years we tried different treatments. He would get better and then worse again.

We found that he was very susceptible to dust and viral infections would set off his asthma. I have a relative who lives in an old house and several times when Jack has been there he has had wheezing attacks. He was actually rushed into hospital once because he became so bad after we had been there two days.

During this attack he was able to say, 'I can't breathe, I can't breathe'. He was very distressed. We tried the Bricanyl. I didn't know how often to give it to him. I was giving it to him every 20 minutes desperately hoping it would work. I was away from home. I rang up the local hospital and said: 'My son can't breathe what do I do?' They told me to bring him in straightaway. The drugs were having no effect on him at that stage. He had obviously got worse and needed hospital treatment. I felt terrible because I thought that I hadn't recognised it early enough, but I don't know whether it would have made a difference if I'd spotted it earlier.

He doesn't ever talk about his asthma. In the first few years when it was bad we had to keep a very close eye on it. We would talk to him about it and read him stories about it and he was obviously very conscious of what he had but it never became a fact of daily life. He wasn't often overtly distressed about it.

He is a bit careful with himself. He's not a great rough- and-tumble, climb-a-tree, throw-yourself-into-muddy-water child. He's not like that. He can't run like the other children. Even now, when he's so much better he runs for a bit and then has to slow down or stop. I think he's found that quite hard to bear. I tell him that it's not his fault. It's because of the asthma. But he's very sensitive about it.

He loves football. Asthma has never stopped him playing anything. But because he can't run as fast as the others and gets tired more quickly, I think it gives him the sense of being a bit of a loser. I know he gets despondent when he's running around and playing a game and he has to give up quicker than the others. He never talks about it but I can see it in his face. He wants to go on but he can't.

He's getting a lot better now. Even if he gets a cold he seems to be much less prone to an asthma attack. He's on daily inhalers – Bricanyl and Pulmicort. He hasn't had an attack for a year or more.

· AMANDA (AGED 15) ·

My asthma was quite bad when I was young. I didn't have it all the time but when I got colds it would always set off the asthma. It would take me much longer to get over colds and my mum was always worried about this. I was told to eat my breakfast and wrap up warmly and if I had a friend round who had a cold my mum would go mad.

I went through a patch in junior school when I had quite a few attacks. It often happened after sports, especially if it was cold outside. I've always liked sport and I did a lot of dancing in those days – ballet, tap and modern. I never had asthma after dancing. I think that was because it was indoors.

I didn't worry too much about having attacks at school because there were three of us in the class with asthma and everyone knew about it. The ambulance was always coming to take one of us off to hospital because of asthma but it was usually the other two.

I remember one attack where I was scared. It was in the middle of the night. I woke up and I couldn't breathe. I tried my inhaler but it didn't work. I was frightened because the house was so quiet. My parents were asleep and I was afraid that I wouldn't be able to wake them up and explain what was happening. I got out of bed and went into their room. I was gasping for breath. I put on the light and my mum woke up immediately. She took one look at me and screamed at my dad to wake up. She sat me down and made me do my inhaler again. It still didn't do very much. We got straight in the car and drove to the hospital. It's not a very long way away.

When I got to the hospital they made me blow into a gadget. Then they gave me some oxygen and I had to blow into the thing again. My breathing was a lot easier but I felt very tired. I must have been feeling better because I remember noticing how awful my parents looked.

I was given some steroid tablets for a few days as well as my steroid inhaler and my reliever. After that I didn't have any asthma symptoms for a long time and I came off my preventer treatment.

Then I had a minor attack. Well the asthma was minor but the embarrassment was major. I usually take a puff of my reliever inhaler before I do any exercise. I went to the gym with my boyfriend. I didn't want to take my inhaler because I thought it looked naf. I didn't think I'd have a problem because I hadn't had asthma for ages and the gym was indoors. Anyway I was cycling on the bike next to my boyfriend and I was cycling quite hard. We were laughing and having a wicked time and then I could feel my chest get tight. I started to panic and it got worse and worse.

At first he thought I was larking about and then he could see I was in trouble and he looked quite scared. There was someone at the gym who knew what was happening and they asked me if I had an inhaler on me. My boyfriend helped me to where I had put my bag and I took a couple of puffs of my reliever. I sat down while my boyfriend rang my parents. After a few minutes I took another two puffs and I started to feel a bit better.

My mum came and took me to the doctor but I was really all right. My boyfriend rang me that night but I wouldn't speak to him. I felt so stupid.

He came round the next day with some flowers. They were 15 red roses and he'd spent all the money he'd earned that week on them. I had to speak to him then!

10

ASTHMA AT SCHOOL

The 1981 Education Act encourages pupils with special educational needs to attend mainstream schools wherever possible. A child with asthma may have requirements that are nothing to do with learning ability but are necessitated by the condition. In other words your child may need special consideration and you are entitled to ask for it – within reason of course.

The trouble is that many teachers do not know very much about asthma, but it doesn't mean that they do not want to be informed. If your child is attending a new school make an appointment to see the Head Teacher to discuss his or her condition. It is important that the Head understands what asthma is and how it affects your child. The National Asthma Campaign publishes a guide for teachers which you can give to the Head when you leave, but go through the significant points during your discussion.

· *Talking to the teachers* ·

The most important thing to discuss is the question of your child's inhalers. If he or she is taking preventers such as *cromoglycate* four times a day, at least one dose will need to be taken during school hours. Explain to the teacher that this medicine, taken regularly, helps prevent your child from having asthma attacks and therefore the dose at school is a very important one. Children will almost certainly need to be reminded to do this. Most are capable, however, of administering the drug themselves.

Your child will also have a reliever inhaler. It is very important that he is allowed to keep this inhaler with him all the time. Many schools have a policy of locking away children's inhalers. This is an extremely dangerous thing to do.

Melinda Letts, Director of the National Asthma Campaign, comments: 'Nine out of ten teachers do not feel they know enough about asthma. Equally shockingly, in many schools, children's inhalers – their first line of defence when symptoms worsen – are routinely taken away from them and locked up out of their reach.' Writing in the Winter 1994 issue of *Asthma News* she continues: 'There is no excuse for the ignorance that says children might misuse inhalers or that they could be dangerous to other children. We have heard of schools banning inhalers because of fears that they may be used to enhance the effects of glue-sniffing. What kind of school denies asthmatic children their lifeline instead of tackling its own discipline problems?

Most children with asthma are used to looking after their health. They know how to take their relievers when they need them. Those who need preventers as well may need reminding that a dose is due. They will not generally need assistance in actually administering the dose. And if a child has an asthma attack, what she needs more than anything else is a calm, responsible adult who knows that if the reliever does not work within five or ten minutes an ambulance must be called.'

So you are not asking the teachers to be doctors nor are you asking them to administer the drugs. In some Local Education Authority areas teachers are told not to give medicines. Legally, Head Teachers do not have to oversee the taking of medical treatment. You are not asking for this. What you are asking is that the child should be reminded to take his medicine at the appropriate time and that he should have easy, if not immediate, access to his reliever inhaler at all times. Incidentally, the school's medical officer should note the details of your child's condition in the school records.

Another point to stress is that it is important that your child is treated the same as every other child and on no account should he be made to feel that he is a special case or different. There may be aspects of school life that he may have to be more cautious about but the more he can feel an equal part of a team and the same as everybody else, the better will be his state of mind and his studies.

Having established the ground rules with the Head, you need to arrange to see your child's class teacher. When making the appointment, please stress that you will need to spend at least 15 minutes with him or her in private to discuss important matters concerning your child's health. You will not be able to do this in just a few minutes before class or at any other time when there are children around to distract.

When talking to the teacher explain a little about the condition. Stress that asthma is not infectious illness, nor is it a nervous or psychological condition. Stress can trigger asthma as can many other things. (You can point out that stress can trigger many other conditions including, for instance, headaches, migraine, digestive disorders and eczema. It is not peculiar to asthma.) Triggers vary from person to person and child to child and further on we look at some of those which are most likely to crop up at school.

School trips need not be a particular problem to the child with asthma – providing, of course, he remembers to take his inhaler! Make sure that he has one with him and, if you are particularly worried, give a spare one to the teacher in charge of the trip.

Explain to your child's class teacher that some children are very embarrassed about using their inhalers in the full gaze of others, particularly in front of children they do not know very well. The teacher may need to allow the child to use his medication in private, at least until he becomes more familiar and feels more safe in his surroundings.

School teachers with the right attitude to asthma can make an enormous difference to your child's condition, state of mind and academic achievement. Fifteen-year-old Georgie, whose story appears later on in this chapter, says: 'When teachers don't give you special treatment (which you can't stand because it makes you feel abnormal) but know the signs of asthma and can recognise them, you feel part of the school and you feel safe. If I say I'm wheezy my teachers believe me. They never tell me I've just used my inhaler so I must be all right. I know how I feel and I know what I can and can't do. If I can't hand in a piece of work on time they understand. So I don't panic and I do it as soon as I can. When you have that kind of support it makes you determined to do what you want to do in life. You feel nothing can stop you. If I want to do something I go for it. I think that has a lot to do with the attitude of the teachers at my school.'

· *Triggers at school* ·

● **Viral infections (especially the common cold):** When a child with asthma has a cold his susceptibility to an asthma attack rises considerably. This does not mean that he shouldn't be at school, but it should be understood that he is particularly vulnerable. He may need to take extra puffs of his preventer treatment. He will certainly have to keep his reliever inhaler with him at all times. And whereas for children who do not have asthma, exercise in the cold air in these circumstances may not do them any harm, this is not the case for a person with asthma. Exercise and cold air are both asthma triggers in themselves and should be avoided whenever the child is susceptible to an attack, such as when he has a cold.

● **Allergies:** Allergic triggers will vary from child to child. Grass pollen and furry or feathered animals are two of the most obvious at school. Grass pollen can trigger a severe attack in a child who is susceptible. The summer term (May to July) is when grass pollen is at its highest so if your child is allergic to it, he may need to be kept off the grass.

Many children with asthma are allergic to feather and furs and in school these animals will include guinea pigs, hamsters, rabbits and birds. If affected, your child should not be encouraged to stroke or play with them and in fact his susceptibility to them may be so severe that they should not be brought into the classroom.

House dust mites are another major trigger and children with asthma should be kept away, as much as possible, from very dusty areas. Carpets and soft furnishings, particularly old ones are likely to have been colonised by these creatures.

● **Exercise:** This can trigger an attack in some children with asthma, but it is not a reason to stop the child from taking part in sports. Exercise-induced asthma can usually be avoided by taking a puff of *Intal* or *Cromogen*, or, often more effectively, a puff of the reliever inhaler, beforehand. Please explain to the teacher that your child needs to do sports as much as any other child does and they can often be very talented sportsmen.

· *Sports* ·

The aim should be to encourage the child to play as normal a part as possible in life at school. And this includes sports. Obviously there are some children for whom this is not possible. Some children with asthma become very breathless when they run and a puff of the reliever may only help out to a limited extent. But this doesn't mean that they do not want to participate to the extent of their own limitations. If they are not given the chance how are they ever going to know what these limitations are? Six-year-old Jack, whose story appears in Chapter 9, cannot run very fast or very far without becoming breathless but he loves playing football. And so he should. Jeffrey (in Chapter 3) had to prove to his dance teacher that his asthma would not prevent him from doing all the fast dances he so much enjoyed. Had he not had the courage, determination and confidence to get what he wanted he probably would have been limited to slow dancing. He might have found this demoralising to the extent of giving up dancing altogether. Georgie, who suffers from a very severe form of asthma has always been one of the strongest swimmers in her peer group. She is so good at it that she is a member of the group of lifeguards at her local beach. Her story is told later in this chapter.

Of course teachers are responsible for children in their care and asthma can be a very worrying condition. It helps if teachers can recognise the condition, know when it is most likely to occur and know how best to respond to a child with the condition. Here are some pointers:

● If a child coughs a lot after sport, particularly in the winter months, he or she may have asthma.

● Exercise that takes place over a long period of time is more likely to trigger asthma than exercising in short bursts.

● Cold, dry days are more likely to induce wheezing in children with asthma than when the weather is warm and moist.

- Exercising with either the arms or legs alone is less likely to induce an asthma attack that when the whole body is being used.
- Warming up before playing games can be helpful in preventing an attack. Several 30-second sprints over five to ten minutes can protect the lungs for an hour or more.
- Taking prescribed medication before sport can also help protect a child from an exercise-induced attack.
- Swimming is one of the best sports for a child with asthma. It seldom induces an attack unless the water is heavily chlorinated or very cold.
- Encouraging a child with asthma to join in sport is very important, especially if he or she has been off it for a while and lacks confidence in starting again. Being fit can help a child cope better with an asthma attack.
- Pressurising a child with asthma to take part fully in a sporting activity is a bad idea. If he (or she) says he is wheezy take his word for it. Let him sit out and take his medication. If he is not made to feel embarrassed or in some way inadequate for doing so, he will be keen to return as soon as he is fit enough.
- Sports teachers should bear in mind that it takes a lot of courage for some children with exercise-induced asthma to take part in sport. Gasping for breath is not a comfortable situation to be in and many children do sport knowing that it is a possible outcome. A sports teacher who can empathise with this and encourage the children to feel that they are able participants of the sport, without alluding to the asthma, is very special.

· *Pilgrims School* ·

Although most children with asthma can cope very successfully with mainstream schooling, there are a small minority whose asthma is so severe that they cannot take part in school life in the normal way. They may be away from school so often that the chances of catching up, academically, becomes more and more remote. The answer for children in this predicament may come in the shape of *Pilgrims School.*

Situated in Seaford in Sussex, *Pilgrims* is a boarding school for children with asthma and eczema. Founded by the charity Children's Aid Nationwide (ICAN), it is the only school in Britain that specialises in educating and treating children, from the age of nine, with these two conditions. Children who have spent a lot of time away from school in hospital or at home because of either asthma or eczema (or both) may feel isolated. They may lack confidence, feel that they underachieve or are not as capable as others in their peer group. They may also have experienced bullying at school and become depressed and demoralised.

Pilgrims aims to reverse this in children with a severe form of asthma or eczema.

The school has a holistic approach. This focuses on looking at the child as a whole rather than just his or her medical condition. It also includes 24-hour medical cover. There is a well-equipped surgery and a team of trained nurses to provide round-the-clock medical attention with regular checking by a GP and specialists.

There is a strong emphasis on training the children to take their medication regularly. This is part of the school rules. Many children will also attend physiotherapy classes to learn how to breathe normally and to cope with early signs of tight-chestedness in order to increase the chances of preventing an attack.

Apart from the medical aspects, the school aims to allow its pupils to lead as normal a life as possible. Classes are small and, for children who have missed out on a lot of schooling, remedial teaching is both necessary and available. The school follows the *National Curriculum* and students take anything up to 10 subjects at GCSE.

For some children at *Pilgrims* it may be the first time that their asthma has come under control. This may be because they are under constant supervision and they are being seen by the same medical staff who get to know them as people as well as understanding their condition. This may be a very different experience to being under the care of different doctors and nurses at the child's local hospital each time he has an attack. As the condition improves, so does the class attendance and children often catch up on their studies quite quickly. The school also encourages children to take part in sporting activities.

It is difficult for some parents to get used to the idea of sending children away to school. We feel we should be able to cope at home and that our children should be able to attend mainstream schools. Although in theory this true, in practice, for children whose asthma is so bad that they miss out on a lot of schooling, the repercussions of feeling lonely or inadequate need to be considered. One of the most valuable things on offer at *Pilgrims* is for children to see others in the same predicament as themselves. As they watch these children progress and achieve they realise that with effort they can benefit too. They also cease to be different. Here they are the same as the others. In place of isolation is the offer of mutual support

Keeping a child at *Pilgrims* is not cheap. It is estimated to cost around £21,000 per child per year. The school fees are paid by the Local Education Authority in which the child lives. It can be a bit of a struggle to get some local authorities to sponsor the child. Parents have to obtain a *Statement of Special Education Needs* for their child. What has to be established is that the child has special needs – 24-hour medication for instance. Parents who are interested in sending their child to

Pilgrims would probably be best advised to contact the school initially, find out if their child is a suitable candidate, and if so the school will advise parents on how to get in touch with their Local Education Authority. The stay at the school is often for a period of two years but it can be more. During this time children are encouraged to visit home as often as is advisable. The address of *Pilgrims School* appears in Useful Addresses, on page 149.

· GEORGIE (AGED 15) ·

I've had asthma for about 12 years now. It wasn't very bad when I was at junior school. It would affect me if I had a cold or if the weather was cold or sometimes after sport. But I never had any time off school.

When I was 11 years old I joined the lifeguards. I'm part of a voluntary lifeguard team. I'm a strong swimmer and I love being on the beach. A year or so after I joined we were trying to rescue a boat that was full of water. The waves were high and we had to make sure that there was no one in trouble and then sort out the boat. I wasn't qualified to do anything in the water at that time so my job was to do all the running. We didn't have walkie-talkies then so I was running backwards and forwards taking messages to the lifeguard station.

I began to get wheezy but I didn't want to tell anyone because they were busy. I didn't have my inhaler on me. I'd left it behind. I didn't think I'd need it. It was a warm day and up until then I'd been all right. I remember running into the water to help bring the boat out and the next thing I knew I was in an ambulance on my way to hospital. Apparently I'd passed out and gone under water and two of the lifeguards saved me. When my parents came to see me in hospital I was wrapped up in silver foil because of hypothermia. I was on drips and I was unconscious.

My asthma started to get consistently bad about two years ago. At one time I was being rushed to hospital from school by ambulance at least twice a week. I found the attacks very frightening. I'd start to feel wheezy and my chest would then begin to get very tight. It feels like you're suffocating. I used to leave it too late to ask for help. I didn't want to bother anyone. Sometimes I got so bad that I couldn't even talk. I don't do that any more. I've learnt to say that I am going to need help.

One year I was only in school for 12 weeks. I spent the whole of Easter in hospital and a lot of time at home. When you have an asthma attack it takes a lot out of you. You are physically exhausted because you're using all your energy to breathe.

During that time when I was so ill I felt very upset. I was on steroids and I put on a lot of weight which was depressing. I felt I was missing out on everything. I wasn't that worried about the work I'd missed by not being at school because I was in Years Eight and Nine. Year Ten when the GCSEs start seemed a long way away. But I missed going out with my friends. I love swimming but I couldn't go. There was very little I could do. I felt that I was ill all the time and everyone else was healthy. I used to wonder what I'd done to deserve it. Even though there were others at school who had asthma they didn't have it like I had it. I used to wonder 'Why me?' I still sometimes feel like that now but not very often. I've got used to having asthma and these days I lead a very active life inspite of it.

The teachers at my school are absolutely brilliant. They give me a lot of support. Although I've had a lot of asthma attacks at school I've only ever had one bad experience. That was with a new teacher who didn't know I had asthma. During his class my chest started to feel really tight. He started to shout at me saying that I wasn't paying any attention. When he's angry with someone he really lets it out. It came as a shock. I thought he knew I had asthma and he was expecting me to cope. I just walked out of the classroom. But that's the only trouble I've ever had.

All the other teachers have been great. They bought a nebuliser for me. It was during the time when I was always being rushed off to hospital. The nebuliser I needed would have cost about £300. We couldn't afford it. As it was coming up to National Asthma Week the Head Teacher announced that they would do a sponsored swim. Some of the money would go to the National Asthma Campaign and some would go towards buying a nebuliser for me. The children swam for the NAC but when the teachers swam they were swimming for me. They raised enough money to buy me a nebuliser.

It has completely and utterly changed my life. It is a portable one and I take it everywhere with me. I can do everything I want to do because it's there. If I'm at school and I feel wheezy I try my inhaler. If that doesn't work I go and do my nebuliser and then come back to class and get on with my work. When I didn't have it I'd go to hospital and then mum would want me to come home and rest. Now I carry on as normal. I only go to hospital if I am using the nebuliser too often in one day. I'm only supposed to have two nebulisers a day. If I'm using more than that I have to go to hospital and see the doctor because it means that my asthma is out of control.

· GEMMA (AGED 15) ·

I first got asthma four years ago when I was nearly 11 years old. It came out of the blue. We were having an end-of-term test at school. It was an important test and I got very stressed and panicky about it. I tensed up and felt my chest get tight and I found it difficult to breathe. It was frightening because I'd never experienced anything like that before. I was rushed off to hospital and put on Becotide and Ventolin but the Becotide didn't really work for me.

I've had asthma ever since. It almost always comes on when I'm stressed but I also have hayfever and the allergies that trigger the hayfever also trigger the asthma.

At my junior school they knew what to do about asthma. One of the senior teachers had been on a course and she knew how to relax you. She'd massage my back and talk to me about other things to take my mind off it. I found it very helpful and sometimes just being able to relax like that and taking the Ventolin would be enough to control the attack.

My secondary school is a very academic one. There is a great pressure on you to do well. Soon after I came to this school I went through a phase of very bad asthma. During a term in the eighth year I used to come into school in the morning but was sent home before lunch every day because I'd had an asthma attack. During that term I think I only had two weeks when I was in school for the whole day.

I don't know if I was afraid that once I'd get to school I'd have an attack and the thought of that was stressing me out even more. I was worried all the time about catching up on work. Whenever I got to a lesson I'd find that I didn't understand what was going on because I hadn't been there when it was first explained.

Soon after I came to this school I was sitting in a lesson and I started wheezing. The teacher just ignored me. She'd never seen an asthma attack before. My friends asked if they could take me out of the class but she refused. I wanted to get out of the room because it was dusty. I wanted to get into the fresh air. I started to get really bad. By the time she let me out of the room I couldn't speak. They called an ambulance. I was kept in hospital for a week. It was really frightening because I couldn't get the teacher to understand the situation. But that is the only time I have been bluntly ignored.

Some of the teachers are really good but others don't treat asthma as a proper illness. If I'm wheezing I've been told to be quiet. That really upsets me because I try and stay quiet and that makes me worse.

I worry about what other people think of me. If I think I've given a bad impression I get myself all worried. Getting shouted at by the teachers upsets me. I hate being told off because it makes me think I've done something wrong. It makes me feel really guilty.

My friend at school has asthma. When one of us has an attack we are very good at calming the other one down because we know how each other is feeling. When I start wheezing I take my Ventolin to try and stop it straight away. If it doesn't stop I ignore what is going on in the lesson and try and calm myself down. My friends know that they mustn't start panicking. The initial reaction from people is to crowd around you to see what's going on. It makes it worse because you become the centre of attention and you can't explain what's happening. What you need is air. So if I am let out of the classroom I try and get out into the fresh air. I find that helps a lot.

When I haven't got school work to catch up on I love to go out. If we go dancing somewhere I can't keep going as long as the rest of them. But I still really enjoy being out and about with my friends. My boyfriend is always worried that I'm going to start wheezing. If I start coughing he asks if I'm all right and tells me to take my Ventolin. He knows how to handle my asthma. If I'm bad he knows how to calm me down. And I think he likes to know that he's needed.

11

BRITTLE ASTHMA

Brittle asthma is a very severe form of the condition that affects roughly one in 2,000 people with asthma. So it is also rare. People with this disease experience sudden very serious and often life-threatening attacks.

There are two types of brittle asthma. People with the first will not be in control of their condition even though they may be on quite a heavy regime of preventative medicine. There will also be a marked variation in their peak-flow readings during the course of the day. This type accounts for two-thirds of brittle asthma sufferers. Those with the second type will be able to keep their asthma under control to quite a large extent but will still suffer sudden and severe attacks without warning. These attacks can be very difficult to treat. It is not surprising that people with this form of asthma sometimes find it difficult to hold down jobs or lead normal lives.

A higher than normal level of medication is required to try and control this type of asthma. Many patients will be on regular maintenance doses of steroid tablets for long periods of time and most will be using nebulisers to take their inhaled steroids and bronchodilators.

In addition, some clinics use a special pump system which has been found to work for some brittle asthma patients. The pump delivers a continuous infusion of *terbutaline* (a reliever) under the skin. Patients have a small needle placed under the skin, usually on their stomachs. A small tube links the needle to a case which contains a battery-operated syringe. This delivers a constant supply of *terbutaline*. The syringe can be carried in a pocket or in a belt bag. Apparently the pump is generally well tolerated by most patients who use it.

Although it is not known why people have brittle asthma, it has been found that, for patients with the first type of the condition, the triggers are the same as for other asthma sufferers. House dust mites, pollen and furry animals are three examples. Some patients also report a sensitivity to certain types of food – wheat and dairy products being the main culprits.

The emotional side of having a serious chronic condition like this cannot be overestimated. Patients sleep badly and are consequently tired; they may suffer side-effects of the drugs they are taking. If they are on maintenance steroid tablets, for instance, they may put on weight and also be more prone to osteoporosis.

Many patients feel isolated and angry about being unable to control the condition. There is also the constant fear of not knowing when the next attack might happen.

If you have this type of asthma, special medical help should be available to you. This can be through a hospital consultant who specialises in asthma. You may also be able to obtain the services of a special liaison nurse who may see you at the hospital and sometimes at home as well.

· *Cyclosporin* ·

This is a new drug treatment available for some people with very severe asthma. It is only used for patients whose asthma is not controlled by the drugs normally prescribed. It is mainly used for transplant patients as it suppresses the rejection of transplanted organs. *Cyclosporin* is an immuno-suppressive drug which works by dampening down strong allergic and immune reactions. It also has anti-inflammatory properties. It has been used in trials to treat people with severe asthma and has had good results. However there is a downside to any drug that suppresses the immune system and *Cyclosporin* is no different.

People who have any serious infections, suffer from cancer, or who have had cancer in the past are not advised to take this drug. People who have a history of kidney disease, liver disease, high blood pressure, diabetes or high blood cholesterol may not be prescribed *Cyclosporin*. Pregnant women are not prescribed this drug. Perhaps the most worrying side-effect is that it can reduce the efficiency of the kidneys, and taken over a period of time this damage may be irreversible.

An important point to bear in mind is that *Cyclosporin* does not cure asthma: it keeps it under control while you are taking the treatment. Once you come off it the condition tends to reappear.

· *Brittle asthma support group* ·

There is a support group for people with this condition. It was set up by a brittle asthma sufferer called Lesley. She started it because she felt very isolated with this illness. Currently there are 20 members in the group with an age range of 16 to 60. 'I am the only brittle asthmatic in this area,' says Lesley. 'I said to my consultant that I was feeling very lonely. He told me it was very hard because you only get one or two in every area. I decided to write to *Asthma News* and ask if they could find someone who had brittle asthma who I could write to. They put an article in the magazine and I was flooded with letters from all over the country from other people who have been diagnosed with brittle asthma.

So I got in touch with the Helpline (at the National Asthma Campaign) and decided to start up a support group. I organised everybody to write to another person as well as me. Now we all write to each other. We talk about everyday things as well as our asthma and everybody understands how you feel. You don't have to explain every single thing. We are there for each other in our bad times as well as our good. It's as though we all know each other so intimately although we've never met.'

If you would like to be put in touch with the *Brittle Asthma Support Group* contact the National Asthma Campaign. The address is in Useful Addresses, on page 149.

Here are two personal accounts of people with brittle asthma. Bear in mind that this is an extremely severe form of the illness and the stories you will read here are true and accurate, but they are not typical of people who suffer from the usual form of asthma.

· LESLEY ·

I have had asthma since birth. I am 30 years old now. I wasn't so bad as a child. I could go six months without anything and then I'd have a really bad attack. But it wasn't diagnosed as brittle asthma then.

When I was about 10 years old it changed. Whereas before I would be wheezing sometimes for weeks before I had an attack, they now started to come without much warning. They were very hard to control. It was then that my asthma was diagnosed as being brittle.

It's like that now. Sometimes I get warnings but it might only be a niggly wheeze. Sometimes I might know I am going to have a big attack and there is little I can do about it because I don't know when it will actually happen. Other times I can just cough or laugh and suddenly I am wheezing and I can't breathe and that's it.

There are so many different triggers. It can be the weather. I may have eaten something I shouldn't. I'm allergic to alcohol, even in food it makes me wheeze. Food colourings are really bad. But I am into healthy eating.

You get wheezy like in a normal asthma attack. But with brittle asthma it comes on very quickly and it can deteriorate sometimes within minutes. If I'm going to be really ill it is usually in the early hours of the morning. At three o'clock in the morning I will wake up and maybe be a little bit wheezy. I'll go on my nebuliser to try and ease it and if it doesn't work, it's straight up to casualty. Sometimes I've been unconscious by the time I've got there. I've had lots of intensive care treatment. In the last 10 years I've been in 12 times and in seven of those I've been on life-support.

Sometimes you know in your mind that it is not going to clear. I find that there is little point in keeping on putting drugs into your body, taking more and more nebuliser or inhaler when you know deep down that you need something more. Obviously there are drugs the hospitals use that you haven't got at home.

If I am on my own I usually call a friend. Or I phone for a taxi, or an ambu-

lance. Or I phone my dad. He only lives up the road. It depends who I know is available to get me to the hospital. My husband is usually here at nights. And it often happens in the early hours of the morning. I can cope much better during the day. It seems to be much easier to deal with. Sometimes it's very hard to go to sleep. You're breathless and you know you can't manage but you feel that if you can fall asleep it might ease the attack – just being relaxed.

It doesn't matter what anybody says to you. You tense up. It's like a goldfish out of water, you're just struggling to breathe.

I'm very silly about calling for help. I usually leave it to the last minute. I think most of us with asthma are like that. We're not sensible people. We're a danger to ourselves. We think we can cope so we carry on. I think it's not going to get the better of me and I just keep going until something in my brain says I just can't manage and then I get help.

I check my peak-flow. Once the peak-flow starts to dip too far I know I'm in trouble and I need to get to a hospital.

I don't get scared by it any more. I used to. I think I get more worked up when people start to panic. I can't handle people trying to tell me what to do when I know what I've got to do but I just can't do it. Like when you're in hospital, in casualty, they're saying you must sit up straight and breathe. For me I find it easier to sit on a chair and lean over a bed. So I'm all hunched up but it's the only way I find I can breathe.

I feel very sore and washed out after an attack. As soon as I get better I want to get on and do things, but my body is too tired and I have to rest.

During the first three months of pregnancy the asthma was normal and controllable. I only had one hospital admission. It was so much better after that. I could do so many more things. Now that Jessica is five weeks old it is back as bad as it was before. I've been constantly wheezy since she popped out. I haven't been in hospital yet but I know that I'm on my way to a biggy. I can feel it but it's just a matter of taking the drugs and hoping that it doesn't come yet.

I haven't worked for five years because my asthma got too bad. I was having problems getting to and from work because I can't drive. I'm too scared of having an attack behind the wheel of a car because they come on so quickly. I had to give up work. I can't go out to pubs with my friends because it's too smoky. At one time wherever we went I had to be sure there was somewhere I could plug my nebuliser in. Luckily now I have one that runs on batteries so it doesn't matter. I have to make sure I am near a hospital – always.

If I go abroad I have to make sure there is a doctor nearby, or there's a hospital within driving distance. If I have an attack and I can't cope I need to get to a hospital fast. We go to a place in France up in the mountains and the air is as clear and pure as anything. It's in the French Alps. For the first couple of days I'm really wheezy but after that I can go skiing and for long walks – but not up the mountain! I can walk down to the local supermarket to get the groceries on my own whereas here I can't even walk to the corner shop alone. I am quite happy to go out if somebody's with me.

The worst aspect is not being able to do what you want when you want. I have to have somebody with me in case I get half way and I can't manage.

People can be so rude if they don't understand. When you can't breathe you can't talk and if they can't see the disability people can be very hurtful.

I can cope with not being able to breathe. It's the fact of knowing I can't go out. I'd love to go back to work but I can't. It's very hard to have to rely on people when you want to go out. But Martin and my friends are very good and they come round and take me out and help me.

The last time I was in intensive care I was in there a fortnight. It was the worst attack I've ever had. And it came on within 10 minutes of being normally wheezy. I was on a life support machine. I thought I was dead. To wake up and realise that I wasn't dead but was still alive was so wonderful. It was such a great feeling. But it takes it out of you. My dad is brilliant. Whenever I've been in intensive care I've woken up and there he is holding my hand. He never knows what to say. He is so upset by it but he knows that he just wants to be there. Just his being there is more than enough.

After this last attack I couldn't go home. I had lost two-and-a-half stone. I couldn't eat or drink. I was so weak. I had to learn to do everything again. I couldn't come home to the flat with Martin working. I couldn't be on my own. For about 10 weeks afterwards I had to stay with my mum and dad. There had to be somebody there to help me do normal everyday things that everyone takes for granted. I didn't have the strength to wash my hair or clean my teeth properly. It was like being a baby. It is so humiliating at the age of 29 to have to have somebody to do that for you. It was as though I couldn't do anything. That was the worst. Nothing since has been as bad.

But you have to be positive and you have to realise that you come first, not the condition. When I first gave up work I sat indoors and cried my eyes out because all I wanted to do was go back to work. I had to come to terms with the fact that I could never work again. Once I did that I found other things to compensate. I do a lot of cooking. When things get me down I go into the kitchen and bake biscuits and cakes. I freeze them or give them away to friends and that pleases me. During the summer I sit in the garden and admire the flowers. The things I took for granted I now really appreciate. I love to sit and watch the trees changing colour and the children playing outside. I am glad to be alive and part of it all.

· THERESA ·

Theresa first developed asthma when she was 10 years old. She is now aged 20. She used to have very severe eczema, which she's had since birth, but now it is mild. She has suffered from hayfever since the age of nine. She also has a mild form of epilepsy which was diagnosed in early childhood. Theresa is now paralysed through osteo-chronditis (softening of the bones) and a crumbling spine. She believes that this condition may have been caused by taking large doses of steroids for many years to treat her asthma. Here is her story.

One day I was feeling extremely unwell and my mum took me to the doctor who diagnosed mild asthma triggered by a severe chest and lung infection.

He put me on antibiotics which cleared the infection and I was also given a Ventolin inhaler to keep the asthma under control.

The following summer I had a bad spell of hayfever which triggered my asthma quite dramatically. The doctor then increased my inhaled steroid nasal spray for the hayfever and also started me on inhaled steroid treatment for my asthma. The Beconase nasal spray helped a great deal but the Becotide Rotahaler didn't seem to be doing much until the dose was increased. That seemed to keep things quiet for a couple of years.

Although I felt wheezy and tight-chested I never actually had an attack during those first two years. It wasn't until I played my first game of hockey at secondary school that I had an actual attack.

I remember feeling extremely wheezy, much more so than usual. The tightness in my chest was really bad and I had this terrible feeling of shortness of breath. It felt as though someone or something really heavy was sitting on top of my chest and this was preventing me from breathing out properly. At the time I didn't realise what was happening but fortunately my games teacher knew what it was and she knew how to deal with it. She sat me down, helped me take my inhaler and she helped me to control my breathing.

I found this first asthma attack to be one of the most frightening experiences I have ever come across even though that attack was mild compared to the ones I've had since. But I suppose I've now got so used to them. It still scares me, but nowadays I become unconscious during most of my attacks so I'm unaware of what's going on.

Over the years my asthma has gradually got worse. My treatment has been changed, dosage increased and juggled around with so much but it doesn't seem to have made any difference in the long run.

When I was 16 years old I was diagnosed as having severe brittle asthma. Since then I have been in and out of hospital every two to four weeks, spending a lot of time in intensive care and even coronary care. Sometimes I can get away with four or five days in hospital: other times I can be in for seven or eight weeks.

When I am admitted into hospital I am usually given nebulisers and they increase my oral steroids, depending on the severity of the attack. Most of the time I am also put on to drips of aminophylline, Ventolin and normal saline. I usually have to be ventilated as well. This is when they put a tube down your throat and the life-support machine does all the breathing for you.

Sometimes my attacks start with just feeling wheezy, but I usually get the tightness in my chest and I'm very short of breath. All these symptoms can appear within seconds and develop in severity within minutes. I think the worst thing about having brittle asthma is that you never get much warning. One minute I can be fine and then the next I can be fighting for every single breath and I can so easily stop breathing.

On the occasions when I get a warning of an attack I take Ventolin and Atrovent through my nebuliser which I use every day and carry around with me at all times. If that doesn't relieve my symptoms, it's straight to the hospital.

I think the worst aspect of living with brittle asthma is that you can never tell when it's going to flare up. So I can't really plan anything. I just have to take each day as it comes.

Just lately my asthma has become extremely severe. In every attack I stop breathing and become unconscious. I have to have someone with me 24 hours a day in case I have a sudden asthma attack. I'm very scared about having an attack if I'm on my own because I know how severe they can get so quickly.

I find my asthma very difficult to control. I use a peak-flow meter twice a day, morning and night, before I take my treatment. But if I am very low or unwell I do what is called 'Pre' and 'Post' readings. This means I record my peak-flow before and after treatment to see how effective the treatment is. When I have a mild attack or even if I am just very wheezy I usually measure between 60-100 litres per minute. But when I have a severe attack I can't register at all. This means that it's below 60.

When I measure my peak-flow I do three blows and record the best out of three. But when my asthma is very bad or even if I'm just very tight, wheezy or breathless I can only do one blow instead of three. This is because the more blowing I do the more it wears me and it can actually make me worse.

By recording my peak-flow on a chart I can monitor my asthma at home on a daily basis. I then take my charts to the doctor and the hospital and they can see my progress and adjust the treatment. If the readings suddenly dip down it can be a warning of another attack. When this happens I increase my oral steroids as well as the Ventolin and Atrovent and I contact my doctor straight away. All this rarely prevents an attack from starting, but it can often reduce the severity.

I had to give up my part-time job as a check-out operator at a local supermarket which I really enjoyed. This was because my asthma became too severe. I would work two or three days and then be off sick for at least a week – often more. I frequently left by ambulance rather than by my own transport (I rode a moped at the time).

I haven't got what you would call a normal social life for a 20-year-old. I'm very limited as to when and where I can go out and what I can do. I enjoy swimming but I must be accompanied by a very strong swimmer and I can only be in the pool for about 15 minutes. The pool must not be over-chlorinated or overheated as either of these can trigger an attack.

I also enjoy going out for a drink, playing darts, snooker and particularly pool. I rarely get to do any of these things because I must rely on somebody else. I can only go out when the weather is fine which means I don't get out much during the autumn and winter. Also if the atmosphere at a party, pub or club is too hot and smoky that can trigger an attack.

I find relationships with boyfriends very hard. A good relationship will only last about two months for the simple reason they can't cope with my illnesses and disability, particularly my asthma because I'm in and out of hospital so much. And I can't go out very much.

I have to put my health first. I feel there are not many people who understand just how severe asthma can be and how it effects my daily life. Sometimes I'm too breathless to wheel my wheelchair across the room. Joining the Brittle Asthma group has helped a lot. We give each other help, support, advice and understanding and it is comforting to know that I'm not the only one suffering from such a severe form of asthma.

I've got many local friends and relatives who have asthma but they all suf-

fer mildly and don't understand how different it is for me. I don't think any of them have even been taken into hospital for an attack. But the doctors have told me that the day may come when I just might not be able to get medical help quickly enough because my asthma is so brittle. . .

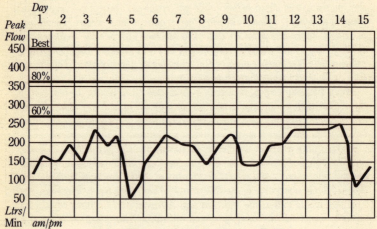

Fig. 4 **Theresa's peak-flow readings**

Fig. 4 shows a peak-flow chart that Theresa recorded over a two-week period. It shows how her breathing dipped suddenly on Day 5 to the extent that she was unable to register a recording before she took her treatment. Post treatment it rose to 70 litres per minute. It shows how with brittle asthma an attack can come on very suddenly.

12

RELATED CONDITIONS

· *Atopic eczema* ·

Atopic eczema usually starts in childhood but can also appear for the first time in adolescence or adulthood. There is usually a family history of eczema or one of the allied atopic conditions – asthma, allergic rhinitis and hayfever. Many people who have asthma have eczema as well and, like asthma, eczema is *never* infections or contagious. You cannot give it to anyone.

It is important to get the condition medically diagnosed. There are several different types of eczema which share some of the same symptoms like rough scaling, soreness, red spots, dryness, blisters which burst and weep and constant irritation. Although symptoms may be similar and routine management is the same, there are special treatments to which specific skin conditions respond, so it is important to see the doctor to get the right medication.

Dry skin

One of the most obvious features of eczema is a very dry skin which is also very sensitive. There may be a rash with little blisters or itchy red patches and these are usually found on the fronts of the forearms, behind the knees and on the calves. These common sites of the condition are a very good way of determining whether it is atopic eczema or not.

When the dryness of the skin becomes extreme it cracks open which is extremely uncomfortable for the patient. When it happens on the backs of the knees it is difficult to walk. At the inside of the elbows or the back of the neck it makes movements with these parts of the body painful. The skin can very often crack at the sides of the mouth, making it almost impossible to talk. The ear lobes are a very common site of eczema in babies and young children. Eczema is a very itchy condition. Although scratching aggravates the symptoms it is extremely difficult, if not impossible, for the patient not to scratch.

Scaliness

In addition to being dry, the skin in a person with eczema is also scaly. This scaliness can be caused by the condition but people without any visible signs of eczema can have a dry, scaly skin. This type of skin condition is inherited and it is thought that people with it may have a predisposition to eczema even though they don't seem to have it.

Lichen appearance

Another recognisable feature of eczema is 'lichenification'. This is where an area or areas of the skin are constantly scratched or rubbed until the skin thickens and looks leathery. It is given this name because the skin is said to resemble lichen which is a microscopic, crusty looking plant-form. The skin can also become darker in colour where there is increased pigmentation. The most common areas for this to appear are the back of the neck, forearms, navel, small of the back, shins and the genital area.

Wet Eczema

Redness of the skin is another noticeable feature of eczema. It is caused by an increased flow of blood to the skin, triggered by an allergen or stress or any of the many triggers that affect a person with eczema, and is accompanied by leaking in the walls of the blood vessels causing fluid to seep into the skin.

Other Features

There are other factors besides skin condition. People with atopic eczema will often feel more cold in the extremities and be sensitive to sudden temperature changes. The sudden temperature change can trigger bouts of scratching. You become aware of your skin and that can set off the itch and resultant scratch.

When the eczema is severe and the skin inflamed there is a rapid flow of blood to the skin to keep it warm. The normal heat control mechanism which shuts down the blood flow to the skin to keep the centre of the body warm is not working properly. So initially when you are exposed to the cold you may not feel it. In fact you may be less likely to feel cold straight away than someone who does not have eczema. But what is actually happening is that your core body temperature is dropping without you being aware of it. And this puts you at a greater risk of getting hypothermia, particularly if you have widespread eczema.

People with eczema do not sweat as easily as people without the condition. This can be misleading because you tend to think that if someone is not sweating they cannot be feeling very hot. With eczema the truth of the matter is that the person may be very hot because of his diminished ability to cool down through sweating.

Cold weather can be a problem because it can make the skin dry and chapped which can exacerbate the condition.

Treatment

As with asthma, the important thing to remember with eczema is to keep it under control. Similarly, this means daily treatment which can take time (more so than with asthma) but pays big dividends. The basic treatment is to keep the skin constantly moisturised and so prevent it from becoming dry and cracking.

The trouble with eczema is that the skin can look good on the surface but it may not be healed completely underneath. It can then start itching and get scratched and cracked and the whole cycle is repeated. So moisturising is very important even if the condition is not presenting a problem at the time.

Bathing, moisturising and treating the skin is the daily routine for most people with eczema. Some may find that water irritates their skin in which case they may need to curtail the frequency and duration of bath times. However, most people with eczema benefit from daily baths providing that the water is warm and not hot, a moisturiser is added to the bath water and a soap substitute is used. Don't use bubble bath – it dries out the skin. Bathing can help replace the moisture that is lost from an eczematous skin and adding a moisturiser to the bath water helps lock that moisture into the skin. There are special moisturisers, also known as emollients, which are recommended or prescribed for eczema.

If you have been prescribed topical steroids, you should apply them before you use the moisturisers. Topical steroids are very often used to treat eczema. They are applied directly to the site of the problem. Apply a small quantity after a bath, or once or twice a day, only on patches of affected skin. Once you have placed the steroid cream on the skin allow it to sink in before you apply the moisturiser, otherwise you will dilute the strength of the steroid.

There are a wide variety of moisturisers on the market and it is usually trial and error that finds you the one that suits you best. Ointments are greasy and give the best results on a dry skin. Creams are not greasy and therefore don't leave the skin feeling sticky. You may want to use an ointment at night and a cream during the day.

Bandaging can be used to prevent scratching, protect the affected area or to allow medication to be well absorbed.

Antihistamines

Taken orally, antihistamines can be very helpful in treating eczema. They do not cure the condition but they can reduce the scratching.

Children have been given quite large doses of antihistamine for many years without there being any evidence that they are either addictive or harmful. But you do need to get guidance from your doctor on dosage. Non- sedative antihistamines are not considered to be of any use in treating eczema; so the sedative version is the one that is needed. Obviously these are best taken at night.

NB: *Antihistamine creams should **not** be used by people with eczema as they can cause an allergic reaction.*

Herpes

People with atopic eczema are particularly susceptible to the virus *Herpes Simplex* which appears in the form of cold sores, usually around the mouth. However, with someone who has eczema the virus can appear on affected areas of the skin and spread quite rapidly – particularly if the eczema is severe. This can lead to a serious condition of eczema known as *eczema herpeticum*. So you should try and avoid physical contact with anyone with a cold sore as the infection is very easily passed from one person to another. Babies are particularly susceptible.

It is important to be fussy about hygiene if you have eczema. Drinking from other people's cups and borrowing other people's used towels is best avoided because of the increased vulnerability to infections like cold sores.

Triggers

These are very similar to the asthma triggers and include the house dust mite, stress, pollens, feathers, animal dander, fungi and mould, some laundry products, wool and tight fitting clothes or material which does not allow the skin to breathe. Diet is more likely to affect children with eczema than adults or adolescents, but some food products can affect some teenagers and adults.

There are ways in which you can cut down the possibility of triggering or aggravating the eczema. Here are some ideas:

● Wear cotton next to your skin. Synthetic or woollen clothes and bedding can cause overheating. Some people can get away with putting woollens over cotton clothes.
● Use soap substitutes, mild shampoos and avoid bubble bath.
● Non-biological soap powders and detergents may be better for you.
● Cotton mitts at night should minimise the effects of scratching.
● Take oral antihistamines to curtail the itchiness and to help you sleep.
● Since dietary factors are not commonly associated with adult atopic eczema, please don't embark on a strict diet without consultation with your doctor or dietitian. Food additives are the most likely to cause

problems – particularly artificial colourings and preservatives. Eggs can affect some people but this is rare and allergy to milk is even less likely.
● Overheating, frosty weather, low humidity, dry air, central heating, air conditioning and car heaters can all aggravate a dry skin and eczema.
● Get to know your own triggers. What sparks off one person's eczema doesn't necessarily trigger another's.

· *Hay fever* ·

Many people experience a persistent discharge from the nose and this is known as rhinitis. If the discharge is thick it is called catarrh. If it is watery it is known as rhinorrhoea. Some people experience symptoms all the year round and this is perennial rhinitis. It can be an allergic reaction or it can be caused by irritants. People with asthma often have rhinitis as well.

Hayfever is caused by an allergy to pollen – mostly grass pollen – so problems tend to occur in the summer. One of the symptoms of hayfever is rhinitis, but hayfever affects the eyes as well as the nose and for this reason is sometimes called seasonal allergic rhino-conjunctivitis.

Hayfever affects one in ten people in the UK. It usually starts between the ages of eight and 20. The most heavily affected are the teenage population. One in six teenagers has hayfever. Men are slightly more likely to have the condition than women. Hayfever appears to be more common in towns than in the countryside and the good news is that symptoms seem to improve as you get older.

Symptoms

Nasal symptoms include mucus which can be either runny or congested. There will be sneezing, itching, soreness and irritation. There will also be the blocked-up feeling and this is not caused by mucus but by an increase in blood flow which causes swelling. Eyes will water and itch and also be swollen and these are the symptoms of conjunctivitis. Patients can also experience a sore throat (pharyngitis) as well as itchy ears and headaches. Unsurprisingly all this makes the patient feel very unwell and one of the outcomes of this is poor concentration. Since hayfever symptoms are most often experienced in the summer, it can be very difficult for student sufferers who are sitting exams at this time.

Triggers

The triggers for hayfever are seasonal. Tree pollen can be a problem for susceptible people in the spring. Grass pollen is at its highest in summer.

Hot, sunny days are those to look out for in particular. Weed pollen and mould spores present problems in the autumn.

What actually happens is that when airborne pollen grains are blown into the eyes and noses of susceptible people, an allergic response is set in motion. This response is the rhinitis, watery eyes, sore throat – in other words the symptoms of hayfever. Flowers pollinated by insects tend to produce heavier pollen which is not airborne and therefore do not present the same problem.

Allergens that are not seasonal, such as the house dust mite and animal dander, can cause perennial rhinitis in people who are sensitive to them.

Avoiding triggers

The first step is, of course, to find out what it is that is causing your symptoms. If these occur some months and not others you can get a fair idea of what is causing them. If they appear in March, April and early May it is likely to be tree pollen that is the culprit. Symptoms that occur from May to the end of July are likely to be caused by grass pollen.

Most grass pollens are released in the morning and rise into the air as the day gets warmer. Pollen can sometimes rise very high. It can be blown for miles so even towns and cities that appear to have very little in the way of grass can have had a lot of pollen blown in from further afield. As evening comes and the air cools down the pollen starts to descend. So in the early evening (between 5pm and 6pm) there can be a lot of pollen around at a level in the atmosphere where it can cause problems. On wet and cool days there is very little pollen around.

To minimise your contact with pollen try to:

● Check the pollen count if you are planning on going out. Pollen is measured at different sites around the country. Pollen is counted in terms of the number of pollen grains in each cubic metre of air. Below 50 is low; 200 and over is high. Pollen counts and forecasts are recorded daily by the media.
● Stay away from long grass.
● Protect your eyes by wearing dark glasses.
● Keep your windows closed, particularly at times when the pollen is likely to be high which is mid-morning and early evening.
● If you are driving, keep the car windows shut and turn off ventilation unless it has a filter which filters out pollen.
● If you are working, studying or sitting exams, sit as far away from open windows as you can.
● Do not mow the lawn yourself and if someone else is doing it stay well away!

• Choose holiday locations that are low in pollen if you possibly can. The seaside is less likely to be pollen-rich than, for instance, mountainous countryside.

Treatment

Hayfever medicine has come a long way and not only can it control most symptoms but many of the drugs do so without causing drowsiness.

• **Anti-inflammatory** preventative treatment is very useful for many people with hayfever providing it is used regularly. Ideally treatment should start before the onset of the allergic season and be kept up until the season ends. *Corticosteroids* are the mainstay of this treatment. These are used as liquid sprays – *budesonide* (*Rhinocort*), *beclomethasone* (*Beconase Aqueous*) and *fluticasone* (*Flixonase*). (The generic name has been given first and the brand name appears in brackets).

Since there is only a small amount of steroids in these medicines, side-effects are minimal but they can include some irritation and, occasionally, nose bleeds. However, if the recommended dose is exceeded more significant side-effects may be experienced.

Sodium cromoglycate can be used very effectively for the nose (*Rynacrom*) and for the eyes (*Opticrom*) but nose or eye irritation can be a side-effect. *Lodoxamide* (*Alomide*) is an anti-allergic eye drop.

• **Antihistamines** are widely used for hayfever. When an allergic reaction occurs, histamine is released into the body and it is this that gives rise to the symptoms. Antihistamines counteract that effect. The following antihistamine tablets help both nose and eye symptoms and cause little or no drowsiness: *acrivastine* (*Semprex*), *astemizole* (*Hismanal, Pollon-Eze*), *cetrizine* (*Zirtek*), *loratadine* (*Clarityn*) and *terfenadine* (*Triludan*). The side-effects of these can include dry mouth, headaches, skin rashes and upset bowels.

An antihistamine which is available as a nasal spray is *azelastine* (*Rhinolast*).

• **Decongestant** nasal sprays can be used to unblock the nose, but they should only be used for a short period of time.

13

COMPLEMENTARY THERAPIES

There are a wide variety of complementary treatments available in Britain. Complementary therapies with their holistic approach have a large following. Treating the whole person and not just the illness in isolation is a very attractive concept and one that brings millions of people knocking on the door of complementary therapists. Many people with asthma may like to try these therapies and there is no reason why they shouldn't do so.

NB: *These therapies must be practised alongside the traditional treatments prescribed.*

Most complementary therapists will go along with this – hence the name 'complementary'.

Asthma is a condition which has to be taken seriously. For some people it is potentially life-threatening. Complementary therapies can be tried if they allow you to keep up with your normal medication during treatment. A therapy that requires you to give up all prescribed traditional treatment may be putting your health in jeopardy and you need to ask yourself whether it is really worth the risk.

Also, bear in mind that there is very little proven evidence that complementary therapies will achieve the results which are sometimes claimed. It should also be stated that the National Asthma Campaign does not recommend any particular complementary therapy, nor does it have any evidence that any of them has been successful in treating asthma.

With so many different treatments on offer it is difficult to know which one to choose. Personal recommendation is a good starting point. If a friend tells you that his or her asthma has improved with a particular therapy, it may be worth a try.

As with other forms of treatment, it is very important to go to a qualified practitioner. There are no laws governing complementary medicine in Britain at present so anyone can set up in practice. However, therapists tend to belong to the appropriate professional body and these usually require that their members have passed examinations and reached the required standard. So unless you are personally recommended to see a particular doctor or therapist, don't pick one at random. Contact the relevant professional body and ask them to recommend one in your area. Also remember that most complementary medicine is not available on the National Health, so it is well worth finding out the likely cost before embarking on a course of treatment.

This chapter describes a very few of the many therapies currently available. The descriptions given here are very brief, so if you are interested in trying a particular therapy it is worth contacting the appropriate professional body to get more information before you give it a try. Relevant addresses are in Useful Addresses, starting on page 149.

· *Acupuncture* ·

The word 'acupuncture' means 'needle piercing'. In China where this treatment is practised widely it is called *Chen chiu*, which means 'needle moxa'. *Moxa* is a dried herb which is burned in small cones on the skin, or on the handle of the needle, to generate a gentle heat. The latter method is known as 'moxibustion'. Both these methods can be used during the course of acupuncture treatment.

Since the needles are so fine, there is no discomfort during the treatment but patients may feel a slight tingling. The needles may be left in for 20 minutes to half an hour or they may be withdrawn immediately.

Children or adults who have a fear of needles are usually given another form of treatment. This includes massage and tapping or pressure with a rounded probe. Alternatively, they may receive electro-acupuncture and laser treatments in which the acupuncture points are stimulated either by a low-frequency electrical current, applied direct with a probe, or with finely tuned laser beams. Gentle electrical stimuli may also be applied through the needles, giving a sensation of tingling or buzzing.

Acupuncture is part of a system of medicine which has been practised in China for several thousand years. More recently it has become widespread worldwide and research has taken place into the whys and wherefores of its efficacy. One discovery has been that stimulation of acupuncture points induces the release by the brain of pain-relieving, morphine-like substances known as *endorphins*.

Acupuncture is based on the principle that our health depends on the balanced functioning of the body's motivating energy. Known as *chi*, this energy flows throughout the body but is concentrated in channels beneath the skin. These channels are called meridians and along them are the points by which the acupuncturist regulates the energy flow and bodily health.

The treatment aims to restore the harmony between the equal and opposite qualities of *chi*, the *yang* and the *yin*. Yang energy is aggressive, representing light, heat, dryness and contraction. Yin energy is receptive representing tranquillity, darkness, coldness, moisture and swelling. A dominance of yang energy in the body is thought to be experienced in the form of acute pain, headache, inflammation, spasms and high blood pressure. An excess of yin can be felt as dull aches and pains, chilliness, fluid retention, discharges and fatigue.

Some GPs practise acupuncture in their surgeries. Others will be able to recommend a qualified practitioner. If you don't want to go through your GP, you can find a qualified practitioner through the professional societies. Since needles are involved in the treatment, the big question mark is going to be hepatitis and AIDS. Members of these professional bodies have to use needle sterilization techniques approved by the Department of Health. These are considered to be effective against the hepatitis and AIDS viruses. Many practitioners use disposable needles.

· *Counselling* ·

A counsellor's job is to look at the here and now and examine current patterns of behaviour. He or she will encourage you to talk freely without fear of being judged or criticised in any way. But the counsellor is also trained to try and relate current feelings and behaviour to experiences that you have had in the past. This will include delving into childhood and family background to try and get a clearer picture of you as a person and what has made you who you are now. Over a period of time, this kind of examination of why you do the things you do can help you see yourself in a new light and help you to understand more about your feelings and motivations.

This talking treatment is good at helping you dispose of some of the unwanted and destructive attitudes and responses – the emotional luggage which many people carry around with them. Counselling can also be useful in current emotional situations. If you are going through a bad patch or unhappy period of your life, talking to a counsellor can help you express your anger and hurt and in so doing, ease the pain.

The point to remember is that counselling is not supposed to be a destructive process – quite the contrary. The aim of peeling back the layers and helping you to know more about yourself is that it should strengthen you, give you more personal power and enable you to feel better about yourself.

With counselling, all this takes place at a conscious level.

· *Homoeopathy* ·

Homoeopathy is the practice of treating like with like. The Greek word 'homos' means 'like'. Homoeopathy was invented in the eighteenth century by a doctor called Samuel Hahnemann who felt that human beings had a capacity for healing themselves and that traditional medicine had its limitations. Hahnemann believed that the symptoms of a disease were a reflection of a person's struggle to overcome harmful forces: the doctor's work should be to discover, and if possible, remove the cause of the problem and to stimulate the vital healing force of nature.

Dr Hahnemann and his followers carried out experiments upon themselves. Over long periods they took small doses of known poisonous or medicinal substances, carefully noting the symptoms they produced (these experiments were called 'Provings'). Patients suffering from similar symptoms were then treated with these substances with good results.

The next step was to establish the smallest effective dose in order to avoid side-effects. To his amazement Hahnemann found that, using a special method of dilution, the more the similar remedy was diluted, the more active it became. He called this method 'potentisation'. However this paradox, that less of a substance could be more effective, was not at all acceptable to scientific thought at the time and Hahnemann and his followers were ridiculed.

These days homoeopathy is much more respected. The principles are still those established by Hahnemann. The patient is treated – not the disease.

Remedies are prepared from animal, vegetable and mineral sources. They are diluted, using the process of potentisation that Hahnemann discovered, so that the patient receives an infinitesimal dose of the remedy which, paradoxically, achieves the maximum effect. There are many homoeopathic remedies used to treat asthma patients and all of these are compatible with traditional medication.

The British Homoeopathic Association can give you more information on this treatment and holds a register of homoeopathic doctors. Some GPs practise it in their surgeries and there are hospitals in various parts of the country which offer homoeopathy on the NHS.

· *Hypnotherapy* ·

In this form of therapy the aim is to shift the client's attention from external to internal awareness. It may sound complex but apparently there are many techniques for achieving this.

With hypnotherapy much of the work goes on in the patient's subconscious mind. The person is put into a trance state. There is nothing weird or mysterious about this naturally occurring state, which is similar to day dreaming or the slowing down, drifting feeling before you drop off to sleep.

Apparently, in the hypnotic state, people tend to be much more receptive to therapy in the form of suggestions and imagery as the left side of the brain, which is in charge of analytical and logical thought, shuts off. So, it is said, the therapist can communicate with the patient's subconscious mind without the blocks and defences that would usually exist. Most clients remember almost everything that has happened while in a trance state.

However, first and foremost a medical history is taken. With asthma this would be along the lines of finding out when the symptoms started. Was there a particular event that set them off? Is there asthma in the family? What are the situations that trigger it? Having established a picture of the condition as it effects the client, the therapist then decides on the course of treatment.

Peter Mirzoeff is a hypnotherapist who describes one of the techniques he uses on asthma patients. 'One of the principle ways I deal with asthma under normal circumstances is to see if there is a fear of an attack. Very often when the person knows that his (or her) breathing is becoming more restricted, he knows that he is going into an asthma attack and he knows what it is going to be like. It can be a fearful experience and very often the problem then becomes the memory. They have the memory of the last asthma attack. And as these attacks continue they build up the fear of the next one.

'One of the things I would work on is that fear. The goal is to enable the client to become gradually more in control and to know that they can be in control.

'One of the best ways of achieving this is by teaching the client self-hypnosis. The person gradually learns to take control over his whole relaxation process. As he practises the self-hypnosis techniques and does it regularly, he becomes more relaxed.

'Eventually when people experience the onset of an attack they can use those skills. They can put themselves into a relaxed state using breathing patterns.'

· *Meditation and relaxation* ·

There are many different forms of meditation and your choice is entirely personal. Yoga meditation is easily available and not at all difficult to learn. Most yoga teachers include it in their classes. Yoga is described later in this chapter. Transcendental meditation is also easy to learn but nowadays tends to be expensive. At the very least, meditation should enable you to feel relaxed and still while you are meditating. Sometimes, if you meditate regularly, this feeling of inner quiet can stay with you, to some very small extent, during the course of a normal day.

Relaxation for Living run classes on relaxation and stress management and also market a series of tapes and books on the subject.

· *Reflexology* ·

Practitioners of reflexology say that they have had some success with treating asthma patients – providing they come regularly and see the treatment through.

As with the other complementary therapies, reflexology aims to help the whole body function more efficiently. The process is based on applying pressure to minute points in the feet. Each zone of the foot corresponds to a different part of the body. This includes limbs as well as internal organs. Through applying pressure on the soles of the feet it is believed that stress-related illnesses can be helped. And it is thought that this happens by releasing endorphins, morphine-like chemicals in the brain.

In addition, if the patient feels pain when the therapist is massaging a certain zone in the foot, it may reveal problems in the correlating part of the body. It is apparently a very relaxing and soothing treatment.

· *Shiatsu* ·

One of the aims of this therapy is to promote relaxation and relief from stress. Shiatsu is a Japanese word which means 'finger pressure'. The theory behind Shiatsu is very similar to that of acupuncture in that the person is believed to stay healthy when the flow of energy circulates unimpeded around the body. Pressure is applied to various parts of the body which correspond with the meridians used in acupuncture. The shiatsu practitioner can apply pressure on the meridians by using his/her thumbs and fingers or elbows and sometimes even knees and feet. This is to stimulate circulation and the flow of lymphatic fluid. It apparently works on the autonomic nervous system, helping to release toxins and tensions from the muscles and, it is claimed, it can also stimulate the hormonal system.

Treatment usually starts with a diagnostic session when the practitioner will examine the person's face which, they say, gives a great deal of information about the state of health. Blemishes, lines and colour changes all have a significance to the shiatsu practitioner. Touch is extensively used as a diagnostic tool and the timbre of the voice is also thought to be an indication of a person's health. Shiatsu practitioners say that they can also diagnose from the pulse.

· *Yoga* ·

Yoga is a system of mental, physical and spiritual development which originated in India three thousand years ago. The word 'yoga' comes from an Indian word meaning 'to unite' and is said to be a means of restoring a healthier balance to body and mind enabling the person to cope better with the stresses and strains of everyday living.

In a yoga class you will probably start by learning a series of stretching exercises which enable the body to become more supple. These postures are not just physical exercises but a way of gaining greater control over body function. Yoga 'asanas' (postures) gently stretch and contract every muscle in the body. Joints are encouraged to move more freely which results in improved posture, and, it is said, greater stamina and vitality.

You may also learn breathing techniques. Yogis have used breath-control techniques for centuries as a means of improving health and vitality. They say that these techniques, practised in the right way under the guidance of a good teacher, can be a means of improving respiration generally.

The classes almost invariably finish with a period of relaxation, when students are taught how to direct the mind to different parts of the body and instruct them to relax. This is followed by a period of deep relaxation.

Meditation is an important adjunct of yoga teaching. Different methods are used to quieten or concentrate the mind so as to achieve an inner silence.

If you are interested in taking up yoga it is very advisable to go to a class given by a qualified teacher. Most of the postures take a certain amount of learning and it is important to get them right. Group classes are not usually expensive and they can be quite social. The *British Wheel of Yoga* is a well established organisation that has qualified teachers who run classes throughout the country.

THE NATIONAL ASTHMA CAMPAIGN

The National Asthma Campaign is the major charity in Britain for people with asthma. It has played a significant role in developing improved asthma management, raising funds for scientific research and conducting extensive educational programmes.

It all started in 1927 when the Earl of Limerick wrote to the press about the distress and suffering caused by asthma. He called for the establishment of an organisation to conduct investigations into the illness. The Asthma Research Council was formed as a result and this was supported by a medical advisory committee with the Duke of Gloucester as Patron. In 1928 the first asthma research fellowship was endowed and Asthma Research Centres established at Guy's Hospital and Great Ormond Street Hospital for Sick Children.

The National Asthma Campaign is a medical charity which was officially formed in 1990 from the amalgamation of the Asthma Research Council, the Asthma Society (which had been formed in 1980) and the Friends of the Asthma Research Council (formed in 1972).

The charity has come a long way since its inception. There are now 160 branches throughout the United Kingdom run by volunteers. Membership is currently well over 20,000 and members usually have asthma or have relatives with asthma, so mutual support is very much on offer. The branches also hold meetings which are open to the public, and speakers tend to be members of the medical profession. Some branches organise swimming groups.

The National Asthma Campaign runs the Asthma Helpline which is staffed by asthma nurse specialists. It is open from 9am to 9pm on weekdays on 0345 01 02 03 and the calls are charged at local rates.

People can join the charity as postal or branch members and they then receive four copies of the magazine 'Asthma News' each year. Members elect the Council of Trustees which is the governing body and the Trustees appoint committees to advise on specialist areas of work.

The aims of the National Asthma Campaign are:

- To promote research into asthma and its allied disorders (this includes funding research projects).
- To provide information, advice and support to people with asthma,

their friends and family, health professionals and other carers.
● To educate the public about asthma and its allied disorders.

Together with the National Eczema Society the Campaign organises holidays each year for children and young people. Described fully in Chapter 8, these holidays can be a major source of fun and encouragement to the young people who participate. They meet each other in a relaxed and supportive setting, take part in a wide variety of adventurous activities and, at the same time, learn more about their condition and how to control it.

The charity also runs a Junior Asthma Club which has its own newsletter '*A for Asthma*'. It is aimed at four to twelve-year-olds.

Since the National Asthma Campaign does not receive statutory funding, fund-raising is a crucial part of the charity's activities. The majority of the spending is on research. In the period 1993/94 £1.9 million was spent on research. Projects for funding are selected by a committee of experts. These include studies around the United Kingdom in universities, hospitals and community health centres. The charity funds 60 or so research projects, as well as two professorial chairs and three senior research fellowships.

The National Asthma Task Force is organised by the National Asthma Campaign and involves eminent specialists from other organisations. They are investigating drug safety and asthma deaths as well as the quality of hospital and community care for people with asthma.

Head Office staff answer about 50,000 written and phone enquiries each year. They produce a wide variety of literature which includes a school pack and video for teachers and a video '*Managing Your Asthma*'. The latter is also available in five Asian languages.

A scheme recently launched by the National Asthma Campaign is the Professional Subscription Scheme which offers all health professionals an asthma information service including a comprehensive range of patient education materials. The Campaign is also launching a professional asthma journal for circulation to scheme members and running a series of conferences and meetings for health professionals.

The National Asthma Campaign has also recently employed a full-time childhood asthma education officer to focus on the development of policies and practices relating to the care of children with asthma. In addition the officer will be responsible for developing and promoting the Junior Asthma Club. The address of the Head Office is given in Useful Addresses on page 150.

A–Z of Asthma

Aerolin is the trade name of an inhaled reliever. Its generic name is *salbutamol*.

Aminophylline is a long acting reliever which is available as a tablet or syrup.

Anaesthetics (general). Anaesthetics should not be a problem for anyone whose asthma is well under control. If your asthma is not under control and you are going to be having a general anaesthetic in the near future, you need to discuss it with your doctor. In any event it is essential that the anaesthetist knows you are an asthma patient.

Asthma is a condition of the lungs in which there is an inherent inflammation of the airways. When a person with asthma comes into contact with an irritant or allergen that he (or she) is susceptible to, the already inflamed airways will become more inflamed and narrow making it difficult to breathe. The airways will become sore and twitchy and can also swell and produce a sticky phlegm. This reaction to substances produces asthma symptoms. Asthma is not in any way infectious.

Atrovent is the trade name of an inhaled reliever. Its generic name is *ipratropium*.

Beconase is the trade name for a steroid aerosol used to relieve the symptoms of hayfever. Its generic name is *beclomethasone*.

Becotide is the trade name of an inhaled steroid preventer. Its generic name is *beclomethasone*.

Becloforte is the higher strength version of *Becotide*.

Beta-blockers can cause breathing difficulties and should be avoided by people with asthma. If you are on them discuss it with your doctor.

Betnesol is the trade name of a steroid nose drop used to treat hayfever. Its generic name is *betamethasone*.

Breathlessness can be a symptom of asthma.

Bricanyl is the trade name of a reliever which is usually inhaled. Its generic name is *terbutaline*.

Brittle asthma is a very severe form of asthma and is also very rare. It affects about one in 2,000 people with asthma. Sufferers experience sudden, serious and sometimes life-threatening attacks. People with brittle asthma require special attention.

Bronchodilators are drugs that open up the airways and help you to breathe more easily. They do this by relaxing the muscles surrounding the airways. They do not protect the airways or prevent attacks. They are called relievers. Quick-acting inhaled bronchodilators should bring relief within about five to ten minutes. The device is coloured blue.

Cigarette smoking causes 100,000 premature deaths every year in the UK mainly from diseases affecting the lungs and heart. Cigarette smoke can induce the airways to narrow and causes damage to the air passages of the lungs that also results in narrowing. Usually the narrowing of the airways in asthmatics is variable in that they are tight one day but can be relaxed the next. In smokers the narrowing can become chronic and difficult to reverse. The combination of smoking and asthma is likely to cause permanent damage to the air passages.

Chronic asthma means that symptoms are often there but it does not necessarily mean that the condition is severe.

CFC-free inhalers are gradually being introduced into the market. These will contain exactly the same medicines although they may look, feel and taste different. They will be kinder to the environment.

Corticosteroids are used to treat asthma and they work by reducing the inflammation of the airways. They are a form of preventer medicine commonly inhaled but are also frequently prescribed in tablet form. Corticosteroids are very different to anabolic steroids used by some athletes.

Cromogen is the trade name of an inhaled anti-inflammatory, non-steroid preventer. Its generic name is *sodium cromoglycate*.

Coughing is one of the main symptoms of asthma. It is a particularly common symptom with children. Coughing at night or with exercise is a frequently occurring asthma symptom.

Depression can aggravate asthma in some people. However depression will not induce the condition in someone who has never had it before. Research studies have linked children with severe asthma to depression in mothers: but so far there has been no news as to which comes first. Does the mother's depression put her child more at risk of having asthma or does the fact that the child has asthma make the mother depressed? As yet we don't know!

Diskhalers contain dry powder and can be preventer or reliever treatment. The powder is sucked in with the breath.

Disability Living Allowance is a tax-free social security benefit for people under 65 years of age who have an illness or a disability and need help with getting around or with personal care, or both. If you are over 65 you may be able to receive an Attendance Allowance for help with personal care. Although there is unlikely to be a medical examination required, you do have to prove special needs to qualify. There are two components to DLA – care and mobility.

If you can only walk a short distance before you feel severe discomfort you may qualify for DLA on the mobility component. Equally, as far as asthma is concerned, if you cannot walk outdoors without needing someone with you to make sure you are safe, you could qualify for this benefit.

You can get DLA for mobility for children who are five or over. This would apply to children who can walk but need someone with them when they are outdoors. They must need a lot more help than children of the same age who do not have a disability.

As far as the care component is concerned you could qualify if you need help with washing, dressing, using the toilet or if you need someone to keep an eye on you. You can claim this benefit for help with personal care for children and babies of any age, but they must need a lot more help than children of the same age who do not have a disability.

For both the mobility and care components you must normally be likely to need help from the date of your claim for six months or more.

If you want to know more ring the Benefit Enquiry Line (see Useful Addresses, page 150).

Disability working allowance provides for people over 16 years of age who are working or starting work but whose income is limited because they have an illness or disability. You need to be working for 16 hours or more a week in paid employment. You may be eligible if you already receive DLA or have been getting one of the following benefits in the last eight weeks: Invalidity Benefit, Severe Disablement Allowance or a disability premium with Income Support, Housing Benefit which includes a disability premium, or council tax benefit which includes a disability premium. You can apply if you have less than £16,000, in savings but any savings between £3,000 and £16,000 will affect the amount of DWA you receive. You can pick up a claim pack to apply for this allowance from a post office or Social Security office (see also Useful Addresses on page 150).

Eczema is a skin condition which belongs to the same family as asthma and hayfever. People with eczema tend to have a dry skin which is very itchy and becomes sore and cracked. Patients can experience extreme discomfort. Many people with asthma also have eczema.

Elderly people with asthma often need higher doses of steroid inhaler to keep them under control.

Exercise often induces asthma attacks in susceptible people. This is particularly so if the exercise takes place outside on a cold dry day or if the patient has a viral infection. People prone to exercise-induced asthma often find that taking a puff of their reliever medicine before exercise is very helpful in obviating symptoms.

Flixotide is the trade name of an inhaled steroid inhaler. Its generic name is *fluticasone*.

Flu, along with other viral infections, is a very common trigger for asthma, so anyone with chronic or severe asthma should consider having the flu vaccine. However, vaccines are very rarely recommended for small children (see under 'vaccine' on page 147) in this section.)

Food does not seem to be a common trigger in asthma. However nuts particularly peanuts, do seem to cause problems. Dairy products, alcohol, seafood, yeast, additives including colourings and preservatives may also cause symptoms.

Genes are chemical codes which are inherited. Researchers are trying to identify the genes that transmit the tendency to react to allergens.

Growth is something that worries many parents of asthmatic children. It is worth knowing that the growth hormone is released in children during sleep and through exercise. Keeping the child's asthma under control so that he or she sleeps well and is able to take part as fully as possible in exercise is important in this respect. Children with asthma sometimes have a delayed puberty and may not reach their due height in their early teens. But they have a longer period of growth which can sometimes go on to their early twenties.

Helpline run by the National Asthma Campaign for people with asthma and their families and carers. Asthma Helpline is staffed by asthma nurses specialists (see Useful Addresses page 150).

Holidays need careful planning as the section in Chapter 8 explains. The NAC/NES joint holiday venture is very popular with children and young people with asthma.

Indoor air and asthma is the subject of a reading list published by the Building Services Research and Information Association. More than 40 conference papers published by the BSRIA examine the evidence and detail the research that has been carried out. BSRIA have also started a two-year sponsored research project into the various test methods for assessing the performance of activated carbon filters, as well as other techniques for removing gaseous pollutants, including smells, from air. The idea is to draw up a draft standard for such filters which would be used by the heating, ventilating and air conditioning industry.

Inhalers are devices that send the drugs straight into the lungs. There are several different types available, some of which are aerosols and others are powder inhalers. Your doctor or asthma nurse should be able to help you decide which device would suit you best.

Intal is the trade name of a non-steroid anti- inflammatory preventer. It is good at protecting the lungs against allergic and exercise-induced triggers. It is very frequently used as a preventer treatment for children. Its generic name is *sodium cromoglycate*.

Ionisers are not considered to be of any value in alleviating the symptoms of asthma.

Irritants like cigarette smoke and other pollutants can inflame the airways of asthma people and cause them to constrict and swell. This in turn induces asthma symptoms.

Junior Asthma Club is run by the National Asthma Campaign. It is aimed at children between the ages of 4 and 12. The club issues a regular newsletter for its members and has a pen pal scheme in operation. More information is available from the NAC.

Keeping reliever medicine ready to hand at all times is essential for people with asthma and this includes children. There are still some schools which shut away children's bronchodilators. This is a very unkind and dangerous practice. If your child's school does this, explain to the teacher that your child needs to use his or her inhaler straightaway when symptoms occur. And they need to be able do this with as little fuss as possible. The National Asthma Campaign publishes a guide for teachers.

Labour rarely induces severe asthma attacks, but if you are worried, discuss it with your doctor or midwife. Epidurals and normal painkillers are considered safe for asthma sufferers. However, if an operation is needed it is essential that the anaesthetist knows you have asthma.

Liaison nurses are a recent addition to the asthma care medical team. They are nurses who may look after you when you are admitted to hospital and will also visit you at home after you are discharged to see how well the treatment is working.

Lung function is to pass oxygen into the bloodstream and to get rid of carbon dioxide which is a waste product. When your airways are constricted, they obstruct the flow of air and in so doing prevent the lungs from functioning efficiently.

Menstruation sometimes aggravates asthma. Some women find that their asthma gets worse during the week before their period is due. This is more often the case with women with severe asthma. If you take painkillers to treat your period pains it could be those which are inducing the asthma (aspirin can provoke asthma in people who are sensitive to it). It could also be due to hormonal changes. If you suspect that a deterioration in your asthma is linked to your periods, keep a recording of your peak-flow readings. If you find a regular drop in your readings before or around your periods, you are probably right in suspecting a link. Stepping up your preventer treatment during this time could keep symptoms at bay.

National Asthma Campaign is the major charity in the United Kingdom for people with asthma.

National Eczema Society is the major charity in Britain for people with eczema.

Night-time asthma can be particularly troublesome because, of course, it can badly interrupt sleep. The worst times are often between 3am and 5am and symptoms include wheezing, coughing and/or a tight chest. It is usually a sign that the condition is out of control – even when the asthma seems to be controlled during the day. If you are having symptoms at night take it as a warning that your asthma is out of control. Your doctor or asthma nurse may suggest that you increase your dosage of preventer medicine.

Nebulisers deliver much larger-than-usual amounts of medicine into your lungs than ordinary inhalers. They are not considered to be safe for unsupervised use at home for most people with asthma. One of the reasons for this is that some people use the nebuliser to relieve an attack but fail to get medical attention to treat what is probably a deteriorating condition. For the majority of people, spacers can be just as effective as nebulisers. But again, if you use a spacer to get you out of trouble, you need to consult your doctor or asthma nurse to find out if change in your self-management plan is needed. People with a severe form of asthma not controlled by normal inhalers may find a home nebuliser useful. Battery-charged portable nebulisers are also available.

Nuelin is the trade name of a long-acting reliever in tablet or syrup form. Its generic name is *theophylline*.

Occupational asthma is the name given to asthma which has developed through the patient being exposed to substances that have induced the condition. The person is likely to have been exposed to these substances for a continuous period of time and the resulting sensitisation is permanent. See Chapter 7 on Asthma at Work.

Oxivent is the trade name of a long-acting reliever. Its generic name is *oxitropium*.

Opticrom is the trade name of a non-steroid hayfever treatment for the eyes. Its generic name is *sodium cromoglycate*.

Passive smoking can damage unborn children. The babies of mothers who smoke develop less well in the womb and are, on average smaller, than babies of non-smokers. If their mothers continue to smoke these young children will breathe in the side smoke from their mothers' smouldering cigarettes as well the smoke their mothers puff out into the room. Breathing in this smoke has a deleterious effect on the lungs of young children who are more liable to coughs, colds and chest infections. They are also twice as likely as the children of non-smoking mothers to develop asthma.

Other people's smoke acts as an irritant to the lungs of adult asthmatics too, and can very frequently induce an asthma attack. Passive smoking causes problems for 60 per cent of people with asthma.

Peak-flow is a measure of how fast you can blow out. Peak-flow meters are used to diagnose asthma but they are also a very useful part of your self-management plan.

Pollution can trigger asthma in susceptible people. If you are worried about the pollution level in your area on any particular day, you can call the Pollution Helpline on 0800 556677.

Prednisolone is a steroid tablet which is used to treat severe symptoms of asthma.

Pregnancy does not usually present a problem. Most anti-asthma drugs are safe to use in pregnancy.

Preventers are medicines that treat inflammation in the airways and therefore guard against the patient experiencing asthma symptoms.

Puffers are also known as metered dose inhalers.

Pulmicort is the trade name of a preventer and its generic name is *budesonide*.

Prescription charges: may be very expensive for you if you require a lot of medicines and it would be well worth thinking about getting an

NHS Certificate of Prepayment of Charges. This way you pay a set amount, either annually or quarterly, and all your prescriptions are covered for that period – whether you have 1 or a 101 prescriptions. To enter this scheme you need to complete form FP95 which is available at pharmacies.

Quick-acting relievers rescue people from breathing difficulties by relaxing the muscles surrounding the airways. They open up the constricted airways. When inhaled, this type of reliever usually works within five to ten minutes and the effects last for about four hours. The device is coloured blue.

Relaxation is a good antidote to stress which can trigger some people's asthma.

Rotahalers are dry powder inhalers.

Rhinolast is an antihistamine nasal spray for hayfever. Its generic name is *azelastine*.

Rynacrom is a non-steroid hayfever treatment for the nose. Its generic name is *sodium cromoglycate*.

Salt may aggravate some people's asthma since there is some evidence that a low salt diet may help some asthmatics.

Scuba diving is one sport that should not be undertaken by people with asthma unless the condition is very mild and you haven't been wheezing in the last 48 hours.

Serevent is the trade name of a long-acting reliever which is usually used to prevent night-time symptoms. It does not replace the quick-acting reliever and should not be used to treat an attack. Its generic name is *salmeterol*.

Sex can very occasionally bring on symptoms and some asthma patients do experience symptoms during intercourse. This can be because of the physical exertion – in which case a puff of the reliever medicine beforehand should help prevent problems. Another cause could be that the activity in the bed releases into the atmosphere extra amounts of dust mite droppings.

Sinus infections can make asthma symptoms worse and so they need to be treated.

Slo-phyllin is the trade name of a longer-acting reliever in tablet form. Its generic name is *theophylline*.

Stress can be an asthma trigger for some people. Although it is impossible to avoid stress, it is important to find ways of counteracting it. You can do this by playing sport, doing relaxation exercises, going for walks, listening to music, reading a good book, meditating – simply taking time off to do things that you enjoy.

Thrush is a fungal infection and can be a side-effect of inhaled steroids. You can try and guard against it by eating live yogurt regularly – make sure the yogurt is labelled 'live' as it is the bacteria in this that helps fight such infections. But also speak to your doctor or nurse about how you take your preventer medicine as it may need to be changed.

Tilade is a non-steroid anti-inflammatory preventer treatment for asthma. Its generic name is *nedocromil sodium*.

Treatment Plans are an essential part of keeping your asthma under control and these need to be worked out with your doctor or asthma nurse. They should involve a normal routine when symptoms are not troublesome and this could be taking daily preventer medicine and using a quick-acting reliever as and when necessary. The plan should include what steps you could take in the event of an acute attack. Part of the plan may also include a follow-up appointment some time in the future to assess how well the treatment is working. You may need to increase medication if the condition is not sufficiently under control or reduce it if the doctor or nurse feels it would be all right to do so.

Triggers are things that induce asthma symptoms. They do not cause asthma.

Triludan is the trade name of an antihistamine used to treat the symptoms of hayfever. Its generic name is *terfenadine*.

Uniphyllin is a long acting reliever in tablet form.

Vaccines for flu are recommended for those with chronic or severe asthma, but not usually for very young children. Vaccines work within 10 to 14 days and it is advisable to have the vaccination in early Autumn. Usually the only side-effect is a slightly sore arm, but some people experience mild flu symptoms for a day or two.

The National Asthma Campaign have had reports of people whose asthma was worse just after the vaccination, but they say that this is very rare. However, if it happens to you, it is important that you discuss it with your doctor when deciding whether to have the vaccination next time. Anyway, you will need your doctor's advice as to whether you or your child with asthma needs to have the vaccination.

Anyone who is allergic to eggs or chicken should check whether the vaccine is grown on eggs. If you have a feverish illness, like flu or a bad cold, you should postpone having the vaccination until you have recovered.

If you are pregnant or feel you might be pregnant, you should tell your doctor as this could influence his advice as to whether or not you should have the vaccination.

Ventolin is the trade name of a quick-acting reliever medicine. Its generic name is *salbutamol*.

Viral infections like colds and flu present a major trigger for asthma, often inducing severe attacks. This is because they damage the airways and increase inflammation. If you have a viral infection you may well need to step up your use of preventer and reliever treatment until you have recovered. It is worth discussing this as part of your self-management plan with your doctor or asthma nurse.

Weather conditions can induce asthma symptoms. Many people find cold dry air a problem. Some find that breezy weather makes them catch their breath. A sudden change in the weather can provoke symptoms in some asthma patients. Many sufferers also find that going out of a warm house into the cold air (or vice versa) can bring problems. Some weather conditions can increase the amount of allergens in the air. For instance, warm weather in the pollen season can create a greater amount of pollen in the atmosphere. Thunderstorms may also induce asthma symptoms in some people.

Wheezing is a symptom of asthma.

X-rays are done on some people presenting with asthma symptoms. This is usually to ensure that the problems are not being caused by something other than asthma. Chest X-rays are more likely to be offered to elderly patients than young ones.

Zirtek is the trade name of an antihistamine tablet used to treat hayfever. Its generic name is *cetrizine*.

USEFUL ADDRESSES

Chapter 5

Quitline
0171 487 3000 (9.30am to 11pm seven days a week).

The Department of the Environment Distribution Centre
PO Box 151
London E15 2HF

Pollution Helpline 0800 556677 (recorded message)

Chapter 6

Regional Health Information Service
0800 665544
(This is a national number: when you phone you will then be put through automatically to your region.)

Chapter 8

Holiday Care Service
2 Old Bank Chambers
Station Road
Horley
Surrey RH6 9HW
01293 774535

Sports Council's Doping Control Unit
0171 383 5667

Chapter 10

Pilgrims School
Firle Road
Seaford
East Sussex
BN25 2HX
01323 892697

Chapter 11

National Asthma Campaign Helpline
Providence House
Providence Place
London N1 0NT
9am to 9pm weekdays
0345 01 02 03 (local call rates)

Chapter 12

National Eczema Society
163 Eversholt Street
London NW1 1BU
0171 388 4097

Chapter 13

British Acupuncture Association
34 Alderney Street
London SW1
0171-834 1012/6229

British Association for Counselling
1 Regent Place
Rugby CV21 2PJ
01788 578328

Relate
Herbert Gray College
Little Church Street
Rugby CV21 3AP
01788 573241

British Homoeopathic Association
27A Devonshire Street
London W1N 1RJ
0171-935 2163

British Hypnosis Research
St Matthews House
1 Brick Row
Darley Abbey
Derby DE22 1DQ

Peter Mirzoeff
(hypnotherapist)
The Old Barn
Town Farm
Beacon Hill
Penn
Bucks HP10 8NJ

Relaxation for Living Trust
168-170 Oatlands Drive
Weybridge
Surrey KT13 9ET
01932 831000

British School of Reflexology
92 Sheering Road
Old Harlow
Essex CM17 0JW
01279 429060

Shiatsu Society
5 Foxcote
Wokingham
Berks RG11 3PG
01734 730836

The British Wheel of Yoga
1 Hamilton Place
Boston Road
Sleaford
Lincs NG34 7ES
01529 306851

Institute of Complementary Medicine
PO Box 194
London SE16 1QZ
0171-237 5165

Chapter 14

National Asthma Campaign
Providence House
Providence Place
London N1 0NT
0171-226 2260 (administration)

National Asthma Campaign Helpline
(9am-9pm weekdays)
0345 01 02 03 (local call rates)

A-Z of Asthma

Benefit Enquiry Line
(For further information on Disability
Living Allowance and Disability
Working Allowance):
Freephone 0800 882 200

ACKNOWLEDGEMENTS

I should like to thank Dr Martyn Partridge, medical director of the National Asthma Campaign, for his invaluable help in checking the manuscript for medical accuracy. I am also very grateful to Dr Imelda Qasrawi and Claire Nixon of the National Asthma Campaign for their expert advice and support. Most of all I should like to thank the asthma patients who so generously gave their time to tell me their stories.

Jenny Lewis, March 1995

INDEX